LEAP INTO LOVE

Living Present To My Purpose On The Planet

A BIBLE STUDY BY
HAVILAH CUNNINGTON

AUTHOR'S NOTE

I always knew God had a plan for others' lives but never felt God could use me. I struggled with learning disabilities throughout my school years, which caused me to have great insecurity about my value and worth. It wasn't until the age of 17, as I was sitting in a car with friends on my way to a party when I heard the voice of God speak to my heart, "There is more to life than this! I have called you. Come follow me." I spoke out at that moment, telling those in the car that I had a call on my life and they were welcome to come with me, but I was going to serve God.

I remember walking into our house when I got home, kneeling by my bed and saying these simple words, "God, I'm not much. I'm young; I'm a girl with no special gifting. But if You can use anyone, You can use me." Now, thinking back to that day, it makes me laugh how I'd hoped the heavens would have opened up, with angels descending and ascending on a heavenly ladder – that didn't happen and I didn't need it to. God heard my cry and He was at work to accomplish His perfect will in my life.

By 19, my twin sister Deborah and I were traveling all over California preaching, teaching and singing at any place that would have us. By 21, we had been in seven different states and Mexico teaching about Jesus and His great plan for this generation!

Now, almost two decades later, I still believe today is the Church's finest hour, if we choose to live with passion, purpose and walk in power. I'm passionate about seeing individuals encounter God in a real way and seek to blow the lid off common misconceptions, personal limitations, and powerless living. My heart and passion is to inspire and challenge others to become all God has designed them to be.

Today I wear many hats: wife, mom, pastor, teacher, author, daughter and friend. My husband Ben and I have been leaders at Bethel Church for the past 6 years in Redding, California. We lead a small non-profit ministry called Truth to Table. Five years ago, we put my first Bible study online to inspire those who followed our travels and ministry. Welcomed with tremendous warmth, it encouraged us to continue providing daily devotionals. To date, 100's of thousands of people have joined our studies from all over the world. Leap into Love is our sixth Bible study.

Most days, you can find us doing something to wrangle the energy of our four young sons: Judah, Hudson, Grayson, and Beckham. We love the outdoors, eating good food, being with friends, and exploring new places. We love family and are building ours one day at a time.

THE PROBLEM
SELF-ABANDONMENT

Surveys about fear indicate the fear of public speaking is at the top of many of our lists. Ironically, the fear of death is closer to the bottom. Yes, that's right. We'd rather leave the planet, then speak on a platform. (I bet some of you are literally shaking your heads in agreement as you read this ... Ha! Caught you!) I can't say I don't understand this. I've had my share of pure panic as I've taken a stage. There's nothing worse than having your most embarrassing moment last for 45 minutes.

Why is speaking in front of people so terrifying? It's not like your life is in danger. I think underneath this grueling task is the idea that having a room full of strangers reject you simultaneously is almost too much for us to bear. Maybe the truth is, we would rather reject rejection before it rejects us. And if you've ever gone through a life-altering rejection, you know it almost feels like you would rather die.

Rejection, at its core, changes us. It alters who we are deep down inside. The earlier we experience rejection, the more it affects our development and ability to live with confidence.

The truth is, everybody wants to be confident. Okay, maybe not the confidence we immediately think of. You know the picture of the girl who runs into a room, her hair flowing in the wind, takes the room by force and captures everyone's attention. No, not that kind of confidence. Rather; the confidence that comes with deep and profound assurance of who we are. The confidence that says, I'm here. I belong here. Your opinion can't make me or shatter me. If I was going to hang out with one person today, I'd choose ME!

 Why is confidence so appealing? Because the way you think about yourself is critical to your life. What if I were to tell you that the way you think about yourself will be the most important opinion you ever receive? The attitude you hold about yourself will affect every relationship in your life.

Your attitude has such a profound influence, it will shape every decision. It will affect the way you view God, your family, your friends, your future, and any significant area of your life.

So, this whole week is designed to help you discover the areas of self-rejection that show up in your everyday life. We'll look at the lies we often believe, our external and internal evidence of self-rejection, and how we process this as connected to our purpose. Most importantly, why did God create us the way we are?

So, my friend, grab your Bible, maybe an old notebook, and a strong cup of coffee. We're going to jump into this big and vital topic. I'm believing for a life-altering, legacy changing, relational healing impartation to come right through these pages into your very life! But, more importantly, the Holy Spirit is going to lead you right into the life He's been wanting to give you.

Let's get started,

Day One
I WANT TO BE MORE CONFIDENT

> *"Confidence is not 'will they like me?' Confidence is 'I'll be fine if they don't.'" - Anonymous*

I was running late.

It's not new news if you know me. I never mean to run late; I just try to pack too many things in at the last minute. Most often, I'm ready to head out the door and I think to myself, *"I should make the bed. It's only going to take a few minutes; I can make it work."* or *"I'll just fill the dishwasher and run it so when I get home, I'll have clean dishes."* I'm not a slow person. In fact, I've often prided myself in how fast I can unload the groceries, pack a suitcase or fold a pile of laundry. But I always assume that everything is going to go perfectly and I'll make it on time.

I often don't.

That evening I was running late. I had underestimated my flight's arrival and tried to squeeze in a quick shower. By the time I was in my rental car, headed towards my event, I was already jeopardizing an on-time arrival. I quickly sped into my reserved parking spot and made my way to the back door. Catching a reflection of myself in the mirrored door, I looked a little disheveled. The shoes I had thrown into my suitcase didn't match the dress I had planned on wearing. It was too late now to change. I would make it work.

Entering the Green Room, I was met by the pastor and her team. She was a beautiful woman. You know the kind of woman who looks flawless close-up. She was ten years older than me but she was holding on to her youth tightly and it was working.

Her body didn't have an ounce of fat. Her lean legs seemed to stretch out in perfect proportion to her sculpted arms. High cheekbones. A big smile. All the things I'd hoped God would have handed out to me. Oh well! I couldn't tell if she had tailored her clothes to fit perfectly or if she just had a body that could wear anything. At this point, it really didn't matter.

Her greeting to me was distracted. I couldn't tell if she was scolding me for being late or if she was busy thinking about other things. Either way, I felt bad. No, it was more than that.

My embarrassment rushed over me.

I felt ashamed.

Ashamed I was late.

Honestly ... I felt ashamed that I wasn't more put together. Like, well ... her.

I felt embarrassed I didn't look like her. If honest, I felt ashamed that I had to bring a dress that was larger than normal because I couldn't squeeze into the dress I had planned on wearing.

Quickly gathering myself together, I grabbed a cup of water and took a big sip. Wouldn't you know it, the moment I took a drink, water slipped out of my mouth running down the front of my dress. I quickly tried to hide it but it was too late.

She saw it. She looked at me and said, *"Drink much?"*

"Drink much? Really!" I thought.

I could feel my face turning red as I grabbed a nearby napkin and began to vigorously wipe the front of my dress. I wanted to burst into tears, run out of the room yelling, *"You're mean!"*

I hated feeling this way. What way?

Stupid. Overweight. Under-educated. Out-classed.

How could I be so forgetful? The wrong shoes. The wrong size dress.

The wrong time to arrive. The wrong weight. The wrong everything.

What's happening deep down, will make its way to the top.

It's a hard fact but what's on the inside of you eventually will find its way out. Like a boiling pot of water. If there is dirt inside, it will rise to the surface.

Proverbs reminds us:

"Keep your heart with all diligence, For out of it spring the issues of life." - Proverbs 4:23 (NKJV)

I don't like it when I'm caught off guard by my response. In fact, I often will do anything I can to avoid the heat. Hoping that my perfectly tempered life will keep the broken parts from rising to the surface. Sometimes it does, at least for a while. But eventually, what's happening deep down will make its way up to the surface and I see what's really going on. It's at this point I have a decision to make.

Will I try and hide the evidence of self-rejection, hoping that if I ignore it, it will eventually go away? Or will I roll up my soul sleeves, get my hands dirty and do the work that needs to be done to train my soul to respond well to the challenges of life?

LIES WE BELIEVE ABOUT OUR INSECURITIES

I don't like to talk about my insecurities. It makes me feel insecure. HA! And bad, too! Like I'm missing something everyone else has. Like the game of Musical Chairs, when the music stops and we scramble for our seat, only to realize there isn't one and we're the one person left standing. The feeling of standing there is vulnerable, embarrassing, like you're no longer included.

I think we're fearful of acknowledging these parts of us; fearful of falling apart. Like a house of cards held up by what I *"want to be true"* rather than *"what really is true."* If we acknowledge this isn't working, what else will it expose in our story? Thoughts bombard me. What if no one can really help me? What if I get stuck? What if I'm judged? Labeled?

It's embarrassing to see the broken parts of us. We don't mind being the center of attention as long as it's positive. But the moment we're the one who is hurting, our stories feel excruciating.

If we finally find the courage to take a good look at the stuff rising to the surface, we often wonder if we honestly have the time and courage to work on ourselves?

What if I find deep down there is something wrong with me? Unrepairable. What if it can't be fixed? Why is this all so difficult? Because we've spent most of our lives trying to cover up our flaws and not acknowledge them. Here are a few reasons I believe we get stuck. See if one sticks.

AT SOME POINT, SOMEONE WILL
TAKE CARE OF THIS FOR ME

I got married at 27. Even though I was told various times throughout my singledom that I didn't need a knight in shining armor, I kept a spot in my life called, *"He'll fix it."* You know those big lies, *"I feel ugly because no one is telling me I'm beautiful."* or *"I'm lonely because I have no one."*

Part of that would be true if a warm body was all I needed. But the fact was, some of my needs were on the inside of *"me."* The ones that seemed to rise to the surface in moments of crisis, or weird moments of silence. Left to myself, I would realize there were parts of me I needed to look at and it wasn't anyone else's responsibility except mine. I had to stop waiting for someone to rescue me from my own insecurities. I needed to dig deeper. I needed to realize that fear was paralyzing me from the very truth that would set me free.

I'M NOT GOOD AT THIS

One of the hardest questions for me sounds like, *"How are you doing?"* I quickly jump in with, *"Oh you know ... I'm busy."* I can keep it simple but when someone close to me asks, *"No, Havilah ... how are you really doing?"* I freeze. I'm good at the chit chat but as soon as it comes to my internal narrative, I'm not really sure. It always takes me a few minutes just to think about what I'm actually feeling. But I know everyone isn't like this. In fact, I have very close friends that are masters at this question. Once the question is asked, they are off to the races. They know exactly what they've been feeling and can pretty much give you a play by play of why. I love listening to them but I'm always left feeling like, *"I'm not good at this."*

The truth is, just because we aren't good at something doesn't mean it's not important. Just because it feels awkward doesn't mean it can't ever feel normal.

I DON'T WANT TO LOOK AT IT

I once had a friend tell me this story. Her infant daughter had woken up during the night with a blow out diaper. She said it was so bad she had to wipe her daughter down and put new jammies on her. As she was holding her, rocking her to sleep, the Lord gently spoke to her heart, *"Nicole that is exactly what I want to do with you. I want to help clean you up."* She said immediately she knew what He was talking about: her abusive childhood. At that moment, she gathered the courage to finally look at the hurt she'd been shoving down for so long. It takes courage to finally look at the stuff that we've been hiding but the voice of God is with you saying, *"We can do this together."*

IT'S NOT SPIRITUAL

Why do I need self-acceptance? It doesn't sound very spiritual. If what you see in the mirror is an example of God's passion and creativity, but you HATE it, how can you really trust Him for your life? You are an example of His most significant work.

THOUGHTS FOR TODAY

☑ What's on the inside of me, will find its way out.

☑ There are parts of me I need to look at that aren't anyone else's responsibility except mine.

☑ Just because I'm not good at something doesn't mean it's not important.

☑ It takes courage to finally look at the stuff that I've been hiding.

☑ I am an example of God's most significant work.

Add Five Minutes to Your Study

 LEAN INTO LOVE

> "And I pray that he would unveil within you the unlimited riches of his glory and favor until supernatural strength floods your innermost being with his divine might and explosive power." - Ephesians 3:16 *(TPT)*

Take a minute and think about what power the Holy Spirit has in our lives if we allow Him. *"Supernatural strength floods your innermost being with his divine might and explosive power."*

When we plug into the source of all life, anything can happen. Anything is possible! No matter what we've been told, we can't change ourselves on the inside. Sure, we can say the right things. We might even stop something negative from happening. But, we can't really change without the power of the Holy Spirit. He is the Change Agent in our world. Only when we start to plug our lives into His love and power do things deep inside of us change for the better.

 TAKE THE LEAP

Take a few minutes to talk to the Lord about your journey: Leaping Into Love. Ask Him to help you understand how to lean into the love He has for you. Take a moment to write out a prayer, asking Him to protect you as you start to dig up the painful parts of your story. Thank Him that freedom is waiting on the other side of this journey.

My Prayer

_____

_____

_____

_____

_____

_____

_____

_____

_____

_____

_____

_____

_____

_____

_____

_____

_____

_____

I HATE WHAT I SEE IN THE MIRROR
(EXTERNAL SIGNS OF REJECTION)

> *"Rejection steals the best of who I am by reinforcing the worst of what's been said to me."* — Lysa TerKeurst

"Oh my gosh! Look at my belly!"

......she said, looking at me from the other side of the room as we sat on our beds. We were roommates that summer and after weeks we were now acting like sisters. The real truth was slipping out.

The sound in the other room was our other roommate energetically exercising with her jump rope; her 30-minute routine each and every day. In addition to her hour run and an evening of crunches, pushups, and sit-ups. She was sixteen years old and she was a stunner. Her naturally curly hair with tips of golden blond matched her bronze skin and her beauty pageant smile. She was the picture of perfection. Even her name was exotic. You got a sense her parents knew that this child couldn't have a normal name. It just wouldn't do.

The voice of my roommate across the room interrupted my thoughts. *"Uggh! This stomach."* I sat there taking it all in, feeling a little guilty that I didn't even think about exercising that day, or any day, for that matter. I was also trying to figure out what my friend was complaining about. Her belly was a picture of washboard abs and health. I sat there wondering what her life would look like if she was already obsessed with her body at the age of sixteen.

EXTERNAL: THE UNIVERSAL BEAUTY STANDARD

It's not hard to understand why we all want to be beautiful. An uninterrupted message from a very young age has been targeting each of us. For those living in the Western world, obsession with appearance begins well before you understand the **damage bombarding your innocent life.**

Glossy magazine covers of photoshopped bodies, expensive commercials depicting the perfect hair, eyes, and skin: aggressive messaging about a *"Universal Beauty Standard."* But it's not just the ideal image that's being propagated. Underneath all of these images is the message that <u>beauty and perfection are the only way we can be truly happy.</u>

If you want others to like you? You better look good.

If you want to be worthy of attention? You'll need to be pretty.

We're told that only way to truly be comfortable in this world is to perfect yourself.

Focusing only on the external appearance of women sends another message: *"The most valuable thing a woman can offer is her looks. Ultimately, a woman's worth is attached to her level of attractiveness. If women meet this ideal standard of beauty, society will accept them as valuable and give them the permission to hold a positive sense of self-worth."*

Today, we're going to explore Five Ways Self-Rejection Shows Up in our lives on the outside. It may surprise you to see how these habits often point to a deeper issue.

OBSESSION WITH APPEARANCE

What does it mean to have an obsession with appearance?

It's when the voice of *"how we should look"* becomes the loudest voice in our lives. Our appearance becomes the value holder. There's nothing wrong with wanting to look nice, to be admired for our beauty, or even have a beauty that adds value to our vocation.

> *The danger comes when our appearance has the final word about our worth.*

The danger comes when our appearance has the final word about our worth. When the way we look becomes the most important value we bring into the world. Even more serious, when our appearance becomes an obsession that drives everything else we do.

OBSESSION WITH APPEARANCE LOOKS LIKE:

- ☑ Looking in the mirror many times each day.

- ☑ Staring at yourself in the mirror or at a certain defect or flaw.

- ☑ Not going out of the house or hanging with friends because you are concerned about your appearance.

- ☑ Only being able to go out in public after you've spent hours getting ready.

- ☑ Spending hours snapping pictures to get that perfect one, and not posting any pictures on social media until you find it.

- ☑ We all have physical imperfections, but you believe yours make you completely unattractive.

- ☑ You constantly compare your looks to others.

The danger of fixating on our looks is that it becomes an endless treadmill of unfulfillment. It keeps us grasping for significance in the wrong place. We will never find lasting value in dimensions of our lives that will inevitably deteriorate.

So, what is an appropriate perspective toward our looks?

Is it ok to want to look good? Absolutely!

Can you be beautiful? Without a doubt!

The danger comes when our obsession over our looks is covering up a deep disgust about how we were created. **Only when we accept the way God designed us and see our value from His perspective, do we discover our true value.**

I'm reminded of the paraphrased words of Jesus in the Book of Matthew....

"Has anyone by fussing in front of the mirror ever gotten taller by so much as an inch? All this time and money wasted on fashion—do you think it makes that much difference? Instead of looking at the fashions, walk out into the fields and look at the wildflowers. They never primp or shop, but have you ever seen color and design quite like it? The ten best-dressed men and women in the country look shabby alongside them." - Matthew 6:27-29 *(MSG)*

 ## WRONG PRIORITIES

There's a story in the Gospel of Matthew where a young man comes to Jesus and asks Him, *"What can I do to get eternal life?"*

Let's read the rest of the story.

"Jesus answered, 'If you want to enter the life of God, just do what he tells you.' The man asked, 'What in particular?' Jesus said, 'Don't murder, don't commit adultery, don't steal, don't lie, honor your father and mother, and love your neighbor as you do yourself.' The young man said, 'I've done all that. What's left?' 'If you want to give it all you've got,' Jesus replied, 'Go sell your possessions; give everything to the poor. All your wealth will then be in heaven. Then come follow me.' That was the last thing the young man expected to hear. And so, crestfallen, he walked away. He was holding on tight to a lot of things, and he couldn't bear to let go."
- Matthew 19: 19-22 (MSG)

I can totally relate to this man. At times, I've gone to God to ask Him something that I already believe I've got covered. It's easy to find scripture to justify my case. But it's only when I really ask God what He thinks, do I find out where my heart is.

Self-rejection shows up in the decisions and priorities we make. If we don't feel worthy, we can often run from thing to thing trying to be needed. If we don't feel seen, we can strive to position ourselves in places or with people we think are important. When we feel replaceable, we can try and create a life that looks irreplaceable.

Let me ask you something?

What if you stopped looking at your busyness as a badge of honor?

What if you stopped finding your value in your possessions, your title, or in some future opportunity, and start to see your value as an unchangeable characteristic you already have?

 ## EXTRAVAGANCE

Have you ever stopped to challenge the idea that just because someone has the money to do whatever they want, doesn't mean they can buy confidence? In a world of bloggers, influencers, the famous, the wealthy, and the powerful, we must never assume self-confidence will lead to self-acceptance, or that self-love can produce self-worth. It's easy to make the assumption that other people's lives are easier because they don't struggle with the things we do.

THE TRUTH IS: An extravagant lifestyle can be a cover-up for self-hatred and rejection. Haven't we all seen the person who was severely rejected in high school pull up in a sports car at the class reunion? We can all relate to wanting to feel important and be admired. *"I'll show them"* or *"Look what I could have had,"* is a narrative we have all played in our minds. But those goals can't heal the hurt of feeling bullied, mocked, ridiculed or discarded.

In the words of Jesus,

"For what will it profit a man if he gains the whole world [wealth, fame, success], but forfeits his soul? Or what will a man give in exchange for his soul?" - Matthew 16:26 *(AMP)*

Having nice things, and living a prosperous life isn't wrong. But, when it's used to cover up soul wounds, it will always leave us empty and wanting.

DIFFICULTY LOVING OTHERS

When we don't like ourselves, it's hard to love others well. Sure, we can sacrifice for them, serve them out of our need, or even express love and affirmation, but if we don't know our own worthiness, we won't be able to love others with pure love. The kind of love that says, *"I know who I am and Whose I am."*

I Know WHO I Am, + whose I AM.

Wounded people always have a root of self-rejection causing them to hurt others. Like the quote, *"Hurt people, hurt people."* They spend their lives on the defense. Only having enough room for people they like, those who have been good to them, or those who have something to offer them. These relationships aren't inherently healthy. These relationships are very volatile and easy to offend. If you tick them off, say the wrong thing, don't show up at the right time, you'll set them off and find their love was conditional.

Often, gossip is just a way for someone to feel powerful or superior. It only shows they have to marginalize others in order to feel better about themselves. It's not the root of real love; it's the root of self-rejection.

Jesus defined what true love looks like,

"Let me give you a new command: Love one another. In the same way I loved you, you love one another. This is how everyone will recognize that you are my disciples—when they see the love you have for each other." - John 13:35 *(MSG)*

 ## EXCESSIVE SHYNESS

There's nothing wrong with living on the quiet side of life. Not wanting to talk to everyone, all the time, can be really normal and how God created us. But the danger comes when our shyness is connected to a paralyzing fear of rejection.

Have you ever noticed? When we fear what others will think of us, it causes them to reflect our attitude of fear back to us. **Sometimes, when we fear others, they fear us.**

Excessive shyness can be a sign of insecurity, lack of confidence, an incorrect self-image and low self-esteem. When you are shy, you feel unsure of yourself in the presence of others.

Some bad experiences during childhood could have caused you to become timid and withdrawn. When you are uncomfortable with other people, you can't talk, express your opinion, or ask for favors. Timidity can destroy your ambitions, your success, and your relationships with others. You may have a positive intention in your behavior, but underneath you are trying to protect yourself from looking and feeling like a fool.

The more often you label yourself as a shy person, the more your subconscious mind will agree and prove to you that you are right.

Think about the words of Paul the Apostle.

"For God did not give us a spirit of timidity or cowardice or fear, but [He has given us a spirit] of power and of love and of sound judgment and personal discipline [abilities that result in a calm, well-balanced mind and self-control]."
- 2 Timothy 1:7 *(AMP)*

The secret to changing our thoughts isn't in trying to stop thinking them. It's running after God's thoughts and partnering with them. Only then can we have the clarity to let go of self-protection and start to live our authentic self: becoming the person God intended from the beginning.

THOUGHTS FOR TODAY:

- ☑ Only when I accept the way God designed me and see my value, can I accept my true worth.

- ☑ What if I stopped finding my value in my possessions, my title, or in some future opportunity, and started to see my value as an unchangeable characteristic I already have?

- ☑ Having nice things and living a prosperous life isn't wrong. But, when it's used to cover up soul wounds, it will always leave me empty and wanting.

- ☑ Holistic love is the kind of love that says, *"I know who I am and Whose I am."*

- ☑ God did not give me a spirit of timidity, cowardice, or fear… but of power, love, sound judgment and personal discipline.

Add Five Minutes to Your Study

 LEAN INTO LOVE

> Jesus said, "I am the true Vine, and My Father is the vinedresser. Every branch in Me that does not bear fruit, He takes away; and every branch that continues to bear fruit, He [repeatedly] prunes, so that it will bear more fruit [even richer and finer fruit]. You are already clean because of the word which I have given you [the teachings which I have discussed with you]." - John 15:1-3 (AMP)

It's easy to forget that our spiritual life is connected to being rooted in God. God is the farmer and our lives are the vines. As the perfect Gardner, He goes into our lives (our root system) and removes anything that will hurt us, anything that will not bear fruit, long-term.

When God exposes a dangerous root, no matter how insignificant it may seem, He knows the danger it can ultimately have.

 TAKE THE LEAP

Take a moment to consider the Five Areas of Evidence pointing to self-rejection. Write down the areas God reveals to you. Ask Him to help you unroot the weeds of self-rejection that will hurt you. Be as honest as you can. It will help unearth the hidden areas of pain in your life.

Evidence Of Self-Rejection:

_____

_____

_____

_____

_____

_____

_____

_____

_____

_____

_____

_____

_____

_____

_____

_____

ABANDONING MYSELF
(INTERNAL SIGNS OF REJECTION)

> *"The way we talk to our children becomes their inner voice."*
> Peggy O'Mara

My husband came home after meeting with a friend. He was on his own journey to open up more, heal more, and learn more about himself. The friend had asked Ben a question that surprised him. *"What were you like as a six-year-old boy?"* Ben took a minute to think about it but couldn't really give a definite answer.

He was now on a mission.

Calling his Mom, he asked her to send him some pictures of him as a six-year-old boy. A few days later, the photos came in the mail. We looked at them together and Ben went into the other room to consider the assignment.

The next day Ben and I had a chance to talk. We both teared up as he talked about the little boy he used to be. I could see it in his eyes. The joy. The innocence. Remembering an old friend you had forgotten about, until you see them in a video or a picture taken years ago. They were there all along, you just forgot about them.

I believe for most of us, our inner voice sounds something like, *"There is more to me than what you see."* Deep down we all know that we have more to say, more to do, more to communicate than what we've shown the world. Life can sometimes feel like a stunted conversation. You know, those thoughts that we can't seem to get what we're thinking to come out of our mouth. Some of this is because we have never been given full permission to be the person God created us to be. Sometimes it's because we don't actually know what's happening on the inside of us. We've been blocked.

NEWBORN BABIES

When we arrive as newborn babies, we land on the planet with all kinds of needs. These needs are natural and innate . . . God-given. Needs are good. They show us we are alive. Our human needs consist of the basics: food, water, shelter, etc. In addition to all of our outer needs, we have internal needs for love, acceptance, and belonging. Every person is born with these desires to live a fulfilled life.

Each of us relied on our caregiver to make sure our needs were met, to the best of their abilities. Some of us had parents who were not capable of taking care of our most basic needs; physical or emotional. You might have had parents who tried their best but you still ended up with deep emotional needs. They were not made to meet all our needs at all times. Most the time they fell short of helping us develop our internal voice. Even the best intentions of a Mom or Dad could not meet all of our developmental needs perfectly. This is because God, who created us perfectly, wants us to know He is the answer to the insecurities, the unfulfillment, the disappointments we experience within.

We are each created by God and given unique personalities, temperaments, giftings, and feelings. If these attributes are blocked by our parents or peers, (whether intentionally or not) we feel anxious and uncomfortable whenever these qualities try to express themselves. We learn early on how to function in our homes, developing defense mechanisms and how to cope from the hurt in our childhood.

Many times, our childhood pain can fester into feelings of abandonment. We lose touch with our true self, bringing on anxiety that morphs into coping strategies that linger even in our adult lives.

Today, we're going to explore five ways self-rejection shows up as unhealthy habits. It may surprise you to see how these compulsions always point to a deeper need.

 ## SELF-CRITICISM

What is self-criticism and why is it harmful?

"Self-criticism refers to the behavior of pointing out one's own perceived flaws. It could be directed towards various aspects of the self, be it physical appearance, behavior, inner thoughts and emotions, personality or intellectual attributes. Failing at something that is important to us, whether it is a relationship, school, or work, can be painful. Most of these experiences jolt us, threatening the very core of who we think we are and who we aspire to be." [1]

The phrase from the quote above that stands out to me is, "The behavior of pointing out one's own perceived flaws." Why do we do this? Our motivation is, "I'm going to beat you to the punch." I'm going to be the first to point out my flaws so when you point them out it will lessen the sting of rejection. If I reject parts of me, then your rejection won't hurt as bad."

Sadly, it has the opposite effect. Not only do we have the outside narrative of rejection, but we now have an internal voice pointing out each and every thing we are doing wrong.

The terrible part is...... Our internal narrative never goes away. It's always with us. There's no relief. No peace.

1 https://explorable.com/e/what-is-self-criticism

But God came to shut down the accusing voice inside of us, protecting the very core of who we aspire to be.

"So now the case is closed. There remains no accusing voice of condemnation against those who are joined in life-union with Jesus, the Anointed One." - Romans 8:1 *(TPT)*

COMPARISON WITH OTHERS

The enemy of our soul tries to convince us that God has cheated us. He tries to tell us that we didn't get what we needed or that there is something missing on the inside of us. Something everyone else seems to already possess.

When we believe this lie, we quickly run to glorifying what other people have or who they are. It's easier to judge someone else's life than to take responsibility for our own. Another way to say it: it's easier to assume everyone else around us feels accepted than to root out our own feelings of self-rejection.

I love how Paul the Apostle says it . . .

"And don't be wishing you were someplace else or with someone else. Where you are right now is God's place for you. Live and obey and love and believe right there." - 1 Corinthians 7:17 (MSG)

FLOATING BITTERNESS

Some people seem to have a floating bitterness. Their real bitterness may, for example, be rooted in their attitude toward a parent who repeatedly humiliated them. They may live a thousand miles away from their parent, yet they flare up with anger when anyone embarrasses them. This can hurt their ability to sustain close friendships because embarrassment/shame is inevitable in this context.

How does this coincide with self-rejection? You may think your pain is in the past or it's only directed to one area of your life, but bitterness is a root. It sprouts in the heart and infects the whole person.

When we have bitterness about the way God designed us, we are vulnerable to self-rejection infecting every part of our thought patterns.

"In every relationship be swift to choose peace over competition, and run swiftly toward holiness, for those who are not holy will not see the Lord. Watch over each other to make sure that no one misses the revelation of God's grace. And make sure no one lives with a root of bitterness sprouting within them which will only cause trouble and poison the hearts of many." - Hebrews 12:14-15 (TPT)

 ATTITUDES OF SUPERIORITY

How could someone who seems so confident have self-rejection issues? If it's grounded in self-rejection, it's a coverup and a compensation for pain.

I think this quote explains it well.

"A person with an attitude of superiority actually feels inferior, but is trying to narrow his field of comparison."

It's easier to belittle those around you in order to cover up areas of insecurity. It's even easier to limit others value so we don't have to acknowledge our own inferiority. But it's all rooted in self-rejection.

The Bible explains the root and fruit of this deceptive attitude.

"Arrogance, superiority, and pride are the fruits of wickedness and the true definition of sin."
- Proverbs 21:4 *(TPT)*

Trying to lift ourselves above the crowd will never increase our value. Value isn't something we get when we step on or over other people. Value is an inside job. It's grounded in self-acceptance. It's grounded in knowing our worth, no matter what anyone else thinks of us.

Trying to lift myself Above the Crowd will never increase my Value.

 PERFECTIONISM

It's healthy to a certain degree to keep improving on what we have done. But when the time spent outweighs the value of the accomplishments, then it is an unhealthy evidence of self-rejection.

"What we call perfectionism is not the same as the pursuit of excellence, though sometimes the lines can blur. When we pursue excellence, we're determined to do something as well as possible within a given set of talent, resource, and time limits. But perfectionism is a pride or fear-based compulsion that either fuels our obsessive fixation on doing something perfectly or paralyzes us from acting at all — both of which often result in the harmful neglect of other necessary or good things." [2]

Perfectionism can point to self-rejection when we are trying to make things just right, so we feel right. It provides a momentary sense of self-importance, at best. We can actually find greater comfort in the Apostle Paul's biblical perspective.

2 https://www.desiringgod.org/articles/lay-aside-the-weight-of-perfection#modal-372-s0jy5h5f

"But He said to me, 'My grace is sufficient for you, for my power is made perfect in weakness.' Therefore I will boast all the more gladly of my weaknesses, so that the power of Christ may rest upon me. For the sake of Christ, then, I am content with weaknesses, insults, hardships, persecutions, and calamities. For when I am weak, then I am strong." - 2 Corinthians 12:9-10 (ESV)

I want you to remember, these are just symptoms. They aren't a life sentence. Self-rejection is a cancer to your soul. You will have to aggressively treat the sickness. But if you stay with God, you can dig up anything you want and plant the stuff you want to grow. The moment you are honest about reacting in self-rejection is the moment you are invited to learn the power of self-acceptance.

I Accept myself without Discouragement, Fear, or Anger.

The power of radical love that's directed right at your heart, and causes your true self to come forth.

THOUGHTS FOR TODAY:

- ☑ Only when I accept the way God designed me, can I embrace my worth.

- ☑ God came to shut down the accusing voice inside of me.

- ☑ It's easier to assume everyone around me feels accepted than to root out my own self-rejection.

- ☑ When I have bitterness in the way God designed me, I am vulnerable to self-rejection.

- ☑ Trying to lift myself above the crowd will never increase my value.

Add Five Minutes to Your Study

 LEAN INTO LOVE

> "Create a new, clean heart within me. Fill me with pure
> thoughts and holy desires, ready to please you."
> - Psalm 51:10 (TPT)

The meaning of the Hebrew word 'create' is to shape and form.
The idea is that God will help us change the shape of our hearts
into one that pleases Him. Much like clay, we need His constant
guidance to form us within, into His image and likeness. We can't
do it on our own. *"Fill me with pure thoughts,"* means pure and
unmixed. The idea is that our thoughts can be mixed, and that's
never pleasing to God.

The Bible says,
**"When you are half-hearted and wavering it leaves you
unstable. Can you really expect to receive anything from the
Lord when you're in that condition?"** - James 1:8 (TPT)

 TAKE THE LEAP

I love how the Message Bible paraphrases the verses right above
this passage.
**"If you don't know what you're doing, pray to the Father. He
loves to help. You'll get his help, and won't be condescended
to when you ask for it. Ask boldly, believingly, without a
second thought. People who "worry their prayers" are
like wind-whipped waves. Don't think you're going to get
anything from the Master that way, adrift at sea, keeping all
your options open."** - James 1:8 (MSG)

If God is really going to lead our lives, then we have to be quick to listen to what He's asking us to do. Today, listen for the direction God is giving you. It may be simple. He might ask you to turn off your music and talk to Him. He may ask you to buy coffee for the person in line behind you. It may be as simple as making a phone call or making dinner. The point isn't in the size of the request . . . it's in the size of our obedience.

Say this prayer: *"Holy Spirit, I want you to lead me today. Where you go, I'll go. What you say, I'll say. Lead me by Your words. In Jesus Name - Amen."*

Today, God spoke to me...

LEAP INTO LOVE LIVING PRESENT TO MY PURPOSE ON THE PLANET

PRESENT TO MY PURPOSE

"Self-rejection is the greatest enemy of the spiritual life because it contradicts the sacred voice that calls us the 'Beloved.' Being the Beloved constitutes the core truth of our existence." — Henri J.M. Nouwen

Have you ever been asked the question, "If you could throw a dinner party and invite five people (who are dead or living), who would you invite?" My list changes but there are a few people that have been on my list from the beginning. A few years ago I was invited to spend a day with one of those people I'd always dreamed of meeting. As I sat in the room, with a bunch of other people, I couldn't take my eyes off of this woman. She was radiating life. She wasn't young. In fact, she'd lived a pretty hard life. But there was something about her that was magnetic. Interesting. Inspiring. Really very beautiful.

After leaving that day, I started thinking about Jeremiah 9, where it says,

God's Message: "Don't let the wise brag of their wisdom. Don't let heroes brag of their exploits. Don't let the rich brag of their riches. If you brag, brag of this and this only: That you understand and know me. I'm God, and I act in loyal love. I do what's right and set things right and fair, and delight in those who do the same things. These are my trademarks." God's Decree. - Jeremiah 9:23-24 (MSG)

Her beauty came from within, her confidence was magnetic. Here was a woman who understood her purpose and knew God. His trademark was all over her. The evidence was a life well lived. His beauty for her ashes. We couldn't help but stare.

I have a simple core value that you might adopt yourself. It's actually quite simple . . .

I want to be fully present to my purpose on the planet.

I want to live wide awake to the plans and purposes God prepared for me in advance to do on this Earth. Nothing more! Nothing less!

So, what will it take for us to live fully present? What does it look like to accept who God created you to be? In order for each of us to fully accept ourselves, the way God created us, we must see the bigger picture of His plan. We can't, by ourselves, figure out the meaning of life. We need a supernatural moment to see what only our spirit can see. We have to go back to our origin, our Creator God, to see what His plan was all along.

I AM PRESENT to my purpose on the planet

GOD'S ULTIMATE PURPOSE

God's basic plan in creating you and I, is to know and experience Him. It's easy to get caught up in so many other things in life, but this is the real truth.

John 17 tells us:
"Eternal life means to know and experience you as the only true God, and to know and experience Jesus Christ, as the Son whom you have sent." - John 17:3 (TPT)

God has never changed his ultimate plan. He created us for a relationship. To know and to be known, and through this relationship, make Him known. God's ultimate plan for us is to be His kids; to be loved and accepted for who we are. We belong to Him.

Remember Adam and Eve in the Garden? What did He do with them? He walked with them. He spoke with them. Communicated. Cared. He created the perfect environment for them, called the Garden of Eden. But through Eve and Adam's free will and powerful choice, they chose to disobey God. This one choice led to the pain we experience on Earth today. But God couldn't just leave it that way. No, He has the perfect heart of a Father. He wanted to rescue us from being separated from Him for all eternity.

He sent His only Son, Jesus Christ, to not just die for the penalty of Adam and Eve's sin, but also the penalty of our sin as well. Once and for all, God made a way where there was no way. Why? Because He wanted us to have life in its fullness. Not just on Earth but for all of eternity. To live in relationship with Him. That is sacrificial LOVE!

John 10:10 in the words of Jesus says,

"But I have come to give you everything in abundance, more than you expect —life in its fullness until you overflow!" - John 10:10 (TPT)

God has been trying to give us back real and authentic life from the beginning of time. He's been making wrong things right. Everything God has and will do, in our lives, will always be on purpose. He has a massive plan for each of our lives on this, His planet.

OUR FULL POTENTIAL

Our relationship with God is only the first half. The second part is that we would experience the FULL potential of Christ working in and through our body, soul and spirit. Having a relationship with God and fulfilling our potential here and now are the ingredients needed to live a successful, contented life.

What does a successful life look like to God? Success in life isn't about who we are or what we have done. God-given success relates to who we are and what we have done with what we have been given. It's reaching our full potential: the best version of the person God created you to be. Nothing more, and nothing less.

"In a palace, you find many kinds of containers and tableware for many different uses. Some are beautifully inlaid with gold or silver, but some are made of wood or earthenware; some of them are used for banquets and special occasions, and some for everyday use. But you, Timothy, must not see your life and ministry this way. Your life and ministry must not be disgraced, for you are to be a pure container of Christ and dedicated to the honorable purposes of your Master, prepared for every good work that he gives you to do. Run as fast as you can from all the ambitions and lusts of youth; and chase after all that is pure. Whatever builds up your faith and deepens your love must become your holy pursuit. And live in peace with all those who worship our Lord Jesus with pure hearts." - 2 Timothy 2:20-22 (TPT)

Here we see that each of our lives is created to be a vessel for God to use. He encourages us to be a pure container for Christ's purpose: to be sanctified.

"Sanctified means set apart, just as much as there are certain bowls and plates that we use more than others, or are set aside to some honorable purpose, so some people are more sanctified and useful to God than others. They are more prepared for every good work than others. We must never think that some Christians are better than others, or that some have passed into a place where they are super-spiritual. However, we must also realize that some Christians are more able to be used by God than others, because they have cleansed themselves, and made themselves more usable to God."[3]

The deep work of self-acceptance is accepting the person God created you and I to be, without disappointment, fear or anger. On the other hand, it's also not about seeing ourselves better than anyone else because of the magnitude of our impact. Whether we produce gold, silver, wood or earthenware, we all have the same value to Him, just a different script. But our united purpose is to be set apart for the purpose God has uniquely given to each of us.

DIMINISH & DESTROY

The enemy of your soul is fully aware of your potential in God. He wants to destroy every part of it. If he can't destroy your potential, he'll do everything he can to diminish it. He wants you to believe that God has cheated you out of what you should rightfully have. (Read Gen 3:4,5)

"Everything of God gets expressed in him, so you can see and hear him clearly. You don't need a telescope, a microscope, or a horoscope to realize the fullness of Christ, and the emptiness of the universe without him. When you come to him, that fullness comes together for you, too. His power extends over everything." - Colossians 2:8-10 (MSG)

Lastly, our hope in accepting who God created us to be is knowing God's not finished molding us into the person He originally intended. We each sense there is more to us and

3 https://www.blueletterbible.org/Comm/guzik_david/StudyGuide2017-2Ti/2Ti-2.cfm

our story, because there is. Think about the words of Paul the Apostle.

"I pray with great faith for you, because I'm fully convinced that the One who began this glorious work in you will faithfully continue the process of maturing you and will put his finishing touches to it until the unveiling of our Lord Jesus Christ!" - Philippians 1:6 (TPT)

THOUGHTS FOR TODAY:

☑ I want to be fully present to my purpose on the planet.

☑ God's ultimate plan is to know and to be known, and to make Himself known.

☑ My potential is reaching the best version of the person God created me to be. Nothing more, and nothing less.

☑ The deep work of self-acceptance is accepting the person God created me to be without disappointment, fear or anger.

☑ My enemy wants me to believe that God has cheated me.

☑ My Hope is in accepting who God created me to be and knowing He's not finished molding me to be the person He originally intended.

Add Five Minutes to Your Study

 ## LEAN INTO LOVE

> "We have become his poetry, a re-created people that will fulfill the destiny he has given each of us, for we are joined to Jesus, the Anointed One. Even before we were born, God planned in advance our destiny and the good works we would do to fulfill it!" - Ephesians 2:10 (TPT)

I want you to take a moment and think about this reality. God, the One who created the universe and every majestic thing you've ever seen, made you. In all creation, you are His masterpiece! As your Creator, He knows what needs to be added or erased in order to make you the finished person He intended. You can trust Him. He won't let you down. Your life is and will be beautiful. Put yourself back on "God's Easel" and purpose and cooperate with Him today.

 ## TAKE THE LEAP

Take a moment to study the word "purpose." Google the definition and write it down. Write out all the synonyms and antonyms possible.

If you want to go deeper, use a Bible dictionary or go to www.blb.com to look it up. See what the word 'purpose' means in the original Greek and Hebrew languages.

My Study on Purpose

Day Five
REFLECTION DAY

RECORD: WHAT HAPPENED THIS WEEK FOR YOU?

_____

_____

_____

_____

_____

WHAT WAS YOUR PREVAILING EMOTION?

_____

_____

_____

_____

_____

_____

THOUGHT: WHAT DID YOU LEARN ABOUT YOURSELF

_____

_____

_____

_____

SKETCH: HOW WOULD YOU DRAW IT?

REFLECT: WHAT ARE YOU INVITING INTO YOUR LIFE WITH YOUR ACTIONS?

_____

_____

_____

_____

_____

CONCLUSION: IN ONE SENTENCE, WRITE YOUR MOST PROVOKING THOUGHT THAT WOULD MOVE YOU FORWARD:

_____

_____

_____

_____

_____

THE PLAN
RECOVERING OURSELVES

Week Two

I was 19 years old when we set out to start a church. A year before we moved, we hosted meetings for those interested in joining our endeavor. I'll never forget the day we huddled in the small modular on the back church property.

A few of our friends and a few new faces joined us to hear the vision that day. One of those friends was a couple who'd been one of my youth leaders, Kenny and Stephanie Wahlberg. They were newlyweds; young, fun and ready for the next challenge. To our surprise, they wholeheartedly jumped in with both feet... moving with us to a new city that year!

They quickly joined our staff. Kenny became our chief administrator and Stephanie, our receptionist. The church grew fast and Kenny and Stephanie were there all along. If the doors were open, they were there.

Kenny was a unique man. He was the only son of a successful restaurateur. He was also adopted, which he always knew from the start. One of the facts we loved about Kenny was he was brilliant, graduating from Yale University a few years earlier. The dichotomy of Kenny mastering a prestigious school and sacrificing to serve our church always seemed so generous.

Kenny was also a detailed guy. He was the person who crossed every T and dotted every I. He loved spreadsheets, to do lists, email reminders, and numbers. He also really loved the Lord! You would see him in the front worshiping fervently almost every Sunday. The successful background and the raw emotion for God always made you feel his authenticity.

By the time Ben and I moved away, Kenny was still serving as a CFO and elder in the church. He later transitioned out to join his wife, Stephanie, in managing their thriving home-business. Which came as no surprise; they were electric together.

Last year, we celebrated my parent's retirement after 20 years of starting and serving that church. We asked Kenny and Stephanie to share a few words that evening. Seeing them on the stage made my heart flash back through years of memories. Now 20 years later, they had seven kids, one of which was beautifully adopted, and were a leading force in their industry. But they hadn't changed a bit! As Kenny got up to share, he said, "As many of you know, I was adopted." The room engaged. "But what you didn't know and what I didn't know was that the majority of my origin is Jewish." The room erupted. It was almost as if every light inside went on! Of course, Kenny was Jewish.

I sat there in my seat, overwhelmed with the idea, and also a tiny bit jealous. Who wouldn't want to find out they came from Hebrew lineage? I watched his face light up as he shared this fact. Grinning from ear to ear, his head tilted back as he laughed with realization.

You could also see a new part of him was settled. As if the missing piece to his life was finally found, making it easy to rejoice with him at that moment.

As I sat there, I began to consider how this information had impacted Kenny. There's something about finding out our origin that settles a person. Knowing where you've come from often helps you understand yourself in ways only that information gives you. We have to see the past and stay present to build a future.

This week we're going to explore your origin. Not only the places you came from on the earth but the origin of how God created you long ago. We'll look at the layers of your humanity, the origin of your personality, and why your features tell a greater story. This week is all about PROCESS!

So, grab your Bible, a cup of coffee or tea, a willing attitude, and let's get started!

Day Six
LIVING DISCONNECTED

> "The only reason we'll ever feel 'off' is that we've disconnected from ourselves. This disconnection creates the illusion that we're lost. It creates the illusion that we're stuck. It creates the illusion that we're oblivious to where we are." - Rob Kish

There is a really funny, popular Christmas movie that has become a tradition for us to watch this time of the year. The movie main character is a man named Clark Griswold, a dad with a wife and three kids, trying to create the perfect Christmas for his family. It shows him taking his family to cut down the Christmas tree. Taking them sledding. Everything he dreams would make a long lasting memory for his family. Only it doesn't go as perfectly as he was hoping. You watch the struggle as he tries to make room for all the relatives coming to visit during the holidays.

One of the big scenes is when Clark tries to put up a full-blown Christmas display on the outside of his home. He spends hours stapling lightbulbs to the front of his house, meticulously placing them on every square inch. He works all day on this project and, when He's finally done, he quickly goes inside to gather his relatives to experience the exciting moment he's been looking forward to. As they gather outside, grandparents, kids, etc., we watch him ask his wife to do a drumroll with her mouth as he sings a crescendoing melody while simultaneously plugging in the lights. It's supposed to be this amazing moment! But, when all eyes are fixed on the house, and Clark is deliriously excited to see the fulfillment of all His effort, he plugs the lights in and nothing works!!! It's a HUGE let down, taking 'the wind out of his sail'.

Clark struggles to plug in the lights a couple of more times and still nothing happens. Finally, after a few awkward, embarrassing moments, the family members make their way back inside and Clark's left trying to figure out what went wrong. We watch him go through all the emotions. He sarcastically laughs and finally his disappointment escalates into kicking Santa across the roof of his home. He is devastated.

Eventually, after watching Clark have a total meltdown, his wife has a revelation. The problem is the light switch in the basement! She walks down and flips it on. Immediately, all the lights outside come on. It's a blinding, glorious, Christmas light display. Clark cries, his family hugs him, and his relatives finally acknowledge his work. At least for the moment.

This so reminds me of us. It doesn't matter if we have a ton of potential, how fancy we look on the outside, or how together we appear to those around us. Ultimately, our efforts are worthless *if we're not plugged into our Source. Only when we reflect our Creator can we live authentic lives and become who God created us to be.*

Let's read this together,
"Even so, every healthy tree bears good fruit, but the unhealthy tree bears bad fruit. A good tree cannot bear bad fruit, nor can a bad tree bear good fruit. Every tree that does not bear good fruit is cut down and thrown into the fire." - Matthew 7:17-19 (AMP)

Here's what we need to remember:

Good fruit will always be connected to good roots.
Bad fruit will always be connected to bad roots.

FACT: The fruit is always in the root.

When you and I are plugged into God and our spirits are fully alive, life works.

You live life present to your purpose on the planet.

When life isn't working, you have to ask yourself the question.

What am I plugged in to?

Sometimes, the illusion of us having light is merely reflection of light coming from those around us. Without them, we'd live in the dark. What happens when you're not around others who know God and are connected in their spirit? Do you stand firm, deeply grounded in yourself, or do you fade quickly, and find you're losing your purpose? It's only in the dark times that we find out whose light we are reflecting.

Living Disconnected

Likewise, we need to be aware of what we are actually plugged in to. Jesus even warns us, **"Make sure that the light you think you have is not actually darkness." - Luke 11:35** *(NLT)*

We need to be sure we're plugged into a source of light that actually comes from God.

2 Corinthians 11:14 (NLT) says, "Even Satan disguises himself as an angel of light."

As King David writes,

"They will be standing firm like a flourishing tree planted by God's design, deeply rooted by the brooks of bliss, bearing fruit in every season of their lives. They are never dry, never fainting, ever blessed, ever prosperous." - Psalm 1:3 (TPT)

Healthy things Grow

Healthy things grow!

When we begin living planted by God's design, connected to His spirit, we live a completely different life. We have life in the deepest parts of our being. We are no longer subject to the world's messaging, dependent on what others say or think about us. No longer needing life to work out just right so we "feel good" about it. We now have an unlimited source of comfort, connection, and confidence coming from the inside of us.

Jesus promised, **"I am the sprouting vine and you're my branches. As you live in union with me as your source, fruitfulness will stream from within you—but when you live separated from me you are powerless. If a person is separated from me, he is discarded; such branches are gathered up and thrown into the fire to be burned. But if you live in life-union with me and if my words live powerfully within you—then you can ask whatever you desire and it will be done. When your lives bear abundant fruit, you demonstrate that you are my mature disciples who glorify my Father!"** - John 15:5-8 (TPT)

Look at the words of Jesus. **"I'm the...vine and you're my branches."**

He is explaining our original design. He's showing us how everything was meant to work together . . . where we end and Christ begins. He's giving us a way to live fully awake to our potential. Right now!

Without me = No THing With me = Anything

Simply, He's saying:

How do we know we can do anything He's given us to do? Paul reminds us,

"I can do all this through Him who gives me strength." - Philippians 4:13 (NIV)

I love how The Passion Translation communicates it.

"For I'm trained in the secret of overcoming all things, whether in fullness or in hunger. And I find that the strength of Christ's explosive power infuses me to conquer every difficulty." - Philippians 4:13 (TPT)

"Christ's explosive power infuses me." Wow, that's incredible! So when we're plugged into our source, we live with access to explosive power. The same power Jesus had access to on the Earth.

Remember these words in Romans.

"But if God himself has taken up residence in your life, you can hardly be thinking more of yourself than of him. Anyone, of course, who has not welcomed this invisible but clearly present God, the Spirit of Christ, won't know what we're talking about. But for you who welcome him, in whom he dwells—even though you still experience all the limitations of sin—you yourself experience life on God's terms. It stands to reason, doesn't it, that if the alive-and-present God who raised Jesus from the dead moves into your life, he'll do the same thing in you that he did in Jesus, bringing you alive to himself? When God lives and breathes in you (and he does, as surely as he did in Jesus), you are delivered from that dead life. With his Spirit living in you, your body will be as alive as Christ's!" - Romans 8:11 (MSG)

Look at that last part again.

"When God lives and breathes in you (and he does, as surely as he did in Jesus), you are delivered from that dead life. With his Spirit living in you, your body will be as alive as Christ's!" When the Spirit of God is our source, we have an unlimited supply of everything we need.

Jesus is the root of our lives.

He is the root of our past.

He is the root of our future.

He is continually called the Root in scripture.

The Old Testament, speaking of Jesus, says, "A shoot will come up from the stem of Jesse; from his roots, a Branch will bear fruit." - Isaiah 11:1 (NIV)

You can read the whole thing in context verses 1 - 11.

And again in the Book of Isaiah.
"For He [the Servant of God] grew up before Him like a tender shoot (plant), and like a root out of dry ground; He has no stately form or majestic splendor that we would look at Him, Nor [handsome] appearance that we would be attracted to Him." - Isaiah 53:2 (AMP)

In the future, Jesus is called the root of the Book of David in Revelation.

Then one of the [twenty-four] elders said to me, "Stop weeping! Look closely, the Lion of the tribe of Judah, the Root of David, has overcome and conquered! He can open the scroll and [break] its seven seals." - Revelation 5:5 (AMP)

And finally . . .

"I, Jesus, have sent My angel to testify to you and to give you assurance of these things for the churches. I am the Root (the Source, the Life) and the Offspring of David, the radiant and bright Morning Star." - Revelation 22:16 (AMP)

I think this is pretty clear ...

"I am the Root (the Source, the Life)"

Why is this so important?

Because without having Jesus as the center of our life, the source of all things, the beginning and the end of our story, we will live disconnected from the source of all life. Without Jesus, our lives will deteriorate quickly.

"The desire to have integrity will deteriorate to critical perfectionism.

The desire to be loved will deteriorate into a need to be needed.

The desire to be valuable will deteriorate into chasing after success.

The desire to be oneself will deteriorate into self-indulgence.

The desire to be competent will deteriorate into useless specialization.

The desire to be secure will deteriorate into an attachment to beliefs.

The desire to protect oneself will deteriorate into constant fighting.

The desire to be at peace will deteriorate into stubborn neglectfulness." [4]

4 The Wisdom of the Enneagram by Don Richard Riso and Russ Hudson (pg 33)

THOUGHTS FOR TODAY:

☑ When I'm not plugged into the source, I can't live authentic to whom I was created to be.

☑ The fruit is always in the root.

☑ Healthy things grow!

☑ When I begin living planted by God's design, connected to His spirit, I live a completely different life.

☑ I have an unlimited source of comfort, connection, and confidence coming from the inside of me.

☑ Without having Jesus as the center of my life, I will live disconnected and my life deteriorates quickly.

Add Five Minutes to Your Study

 LEAN INTO LOVE

> "Do you see what this means—all these pioneers who blazed the way, all these veterans cheering us on? It means we'd better get on with it. Strip down, start running—and never quit! No extra spiritual fat, no parasitic sins. Keep your eyes on Jesus, who both began and finished this race we're in. Study how he did it. Because he never lost sight of where he was headed—that exhilarating finish in and with God—he could put up with anything along the way: Cross, shame, whatever. And now he's there, in the place of honor, right alongside God. When you find yourselves flagging in your faith, go over that story again, item by item, that long litany of hostility he plowed through. That will shoot adrenaline into your souls!" - Hebrews 12:1-3 (MSG)

Take a moment today to think about this last phrase,

"When you find yourselves flagging in your faith, go over that story again, item by item, that long litany of hostility he plowed through.."

Often our disconnect comes from forgetting the point. We get lost running here and there, busy building the kingdom, and forget we are the kingdom. Hebrews 12 challenges us to go over the story again, item by item.

We also disconnect because we forget how our own personal picture connects to the big picture. Sometimes we have to change the "Us" and "We" to "Me" and "I" and remember the significance we personally have to the story.

 TAKE THE LEAP

Take a moment to journal your story of salvation. You may have never thought about doing this but it's a really great way to stir up the passion inside of us. The Bible says we defeat our enemy by the Blood of the Lamb (what Jesus did on the Cross) and the word of our testimony. Our story in God is our secret weapon to destroy the works of the Devil: to live overcoming, victorious lives.

My Story of Salvation...

_____

_____

_____

_____

_____

_____

_____

_____

_____

_____

_____

_____

_____

_____

_____

_____

_____

_____

_____

_____

Day Seven
THE CORE OF ME

> "Confidence isn't walking into a room with your nose in the air, thinking you're better than everybody else. It's walking into a room and not having to compare yourself with anyone in the first place." - Anonymous

It wasn't until I hit a major crisis in my life until I stopped to think, "There may be more to me than what I know." It was after the birth of my second son, Hudson. The pregnancy, childbirth and beginning days of being a Mom of two was quickly speeding up. I thought everything was normal. Life felt hard but what isn't hard after two pregnancies, two C-sections and two sons under the age of two? Normal. Right? Well ... sort of.

Life felt like I was trying to run through water, but I couldn't get anywhere. The idea of just taking a shower seemed like a life-crushing task. My goal was simple, "Make it through the day." I didn't know how bad it was until I was standing at my son's doctor appointment, unloading everything I was feeling to the pediatrician. After I took a breath, she looked at me and said, "You seem like a rather competent person. It sounds like you may have postpartum depression." As soon as the words left her mouth, my eyes filled up with tears and began to stream down my face. Have you ever had that experience when someone acknowledges something you didn't even know was happening? Pure comfort. She was right. I wasn't OK.

The words of Jesus ring true, **"For if you embrace the truth, it will release more freedom into your lives."** - John 8:32 (TPT)

In the following months, I began to meet with a Christian counselor every week, faithfully. It was one of the hardest things I'd ever done up until that point. Day after day, I would get myself out of my emotional bed and do the work needed to climb out of debilitating depression. There was no secret sauce. Just a lot of internal work to choose the right thoughts, heal my emotions, and partner with the Holy Spirit in a new dependency I'd never known.

Self-awareness is the gateway to breakthrough.

Why is this important? Because if we don't know what's happening on the inside of us, we won't have the power or desire to partner with change, and change requires knowledge. Clarity of how we are made and what makes us function gives us the keys to living the best version of ourselves: the person God created you to be.

Authentic SELF ⟶ ME AS God Created ME to BE.

Think about the words in Psalms.

"I thank you, God, for making me so mysteriously complex! Everything you do is marvelously breathtaking. It simply amazes me to think about it! How thoroughly you know me, Lord! You even formed every bone in my body when you created me in the secret place, carefully, skillfully shaping me from nothing to something." - Psalm 139:14-15 (TPT)

THE CORE OF ME

The core truth of the Bible, when it comes down to who we were created to be, is that we are much more than our personality. There is so much more to each of us than what most people experience.

I love the words of the passage above, "I thank you, God, for making me so mysteriously complex!" We are complex, but this complexity isn't just a bunch of crossed wires piled like a box of Christmas lights. No; we are complex, but skillfully shaped. The verse before this passage says,

"You formed my innermost being, shaping my delicate inside and my intricate outside, and wove them all together in my mother's womb." - Psalm 139:13 (TPT)

We see right away that God gave us an inside and an outside, separate from each other. The Bible tells us there are three parts to our being.

"Now, may the God of peace and harmony set you apart, making you completely holy. And may your entire being—spirit, soul, and body—be kept completely flawless in the appearing of our Lord Jesus, the Anointed One." - 1 Thessalonians 5:23 (TPT)

Our entire being consists of a spirit, soul, and body. Why is this important to know? Because each of these three parts in you; spirit, soul and body, function uniquely, having distinct needs. It's critical that for us to be self-aware... or better yet, spiritually aware...we need to acknowledge and understand these three areas by focusing on them individually.

Today, I want us to look at our *soul* and *spirit*.

In the words of C.S. Lewis, "You don't have a soul. You are a soul. You have a body." He's right. But even in that, your soul is not the deepest and most authentic part of you. You are a soul, but you have a spirit. Your spirit is your innermost being. It's the place God connects with you, speaks to you, guides you. Your spirit is the spark of the divine, setting you apart from all of creation.

Your soul consists of your mind, will and emotions.

Let's take a quick look at these three things:

YOUR MIND

Your mind is where all your thoughts and intelligence live. It's a place of conscious and mindful living. Your mind contains all your thoughts, beliefs, and biases. It's where we think about life.

What spiritual transformation needs to take place in our minds?

"Stop imitating the ideas and opinions of the culture around you, but be inwardly transformed by the Holy Spirit through a total reformation of how you think. This will empower you to discern God's will as you live a beautiful life, satisfying and perfect in his eyes." - Romans 12:2 (TPT)

Yes, TOTAL REFORMATION! Our thoughts need a complete overhaul! Depending on how long you've been thinking, what you're thinking, it will take some serious determination and renewing of our minds.

Why do we want our mind renewed? Hint: Look at the final sentence in the verse. *"This will empower you to discern God's will ... "* We want a renewed mind, so we know the will of God for our life. Why is the will of God so important to us? So we can *"... live a beautiful life, satisfying and perfect in his eyes."*

YOUR HEART

Your heart is where all your emotions and feelings live. It's a place of subconscious desire. Where life happens. Your heart contains all your memories, images, dreams, and visions. It's where we feel life. It's a place of longing. Can you see why it's important to renew our thoughts? Because where our minds go, our emotions will follow. It all works together.

"Where you deposit your treasure, that is where your thoughts will turn to—and your heart will long to be there also." - Luke 12:34 (TPT)

YOUR GUT

Your gut is where our instincts originate. It's unconscious.

It's the place where all your instinct and intuition live. It's a place of unconscious and direct living. Your gut contains all your impulses, past experiences, and existing knowledge. It's where we understand life.

"Embrace the truth and hold it close. Don't let go of wisdom, instruction, and life-giving understanding." - Proverbs 23:23 (TPT)

These aren't new thoughts to the world around us. Most people are aware they have these three dimensions: head, heart, gut. But as believers, we have an awakened part of us that only comes alive when we begin to live in the awareness of God.

YOUR SPIRIT

Your spirit, the Bible says, was dead and now is alive. Everyone on Earth has a spirit, but only after inviting the Holy Spirit to come live inside of you, do you fully awaken to the reality of your true nature.

"But if God himself has taken up residence in your life, you can hardly be thinking more of yourself than of him. Anyone, of course, who has not welcomed this invisible but clearly present God, the Spirit of Christ, won't know what we're talking about. But for you who welcome him, in whom he dwells—even though you still experience all the limitations of sin—you yourself experience life on God's terms. It stands to reason, doesn't it, that if the alive-and-present God who raised Jesus from the dead moves into your life, he'll do the same thing in you that he did in Jesus, bringing you alive to himself? When God lives and breathes in you (and he does, as surely as he did in Jesus), you are delivered from that dead life. With his Spirit living in you, your body will be as alive as Christ's!" - Romans 8:10-11 (MSG)

It reminds me of an adopted child. They live with the mystery of their origin. They aren't sure what feature is inherited, or is actually uniquely them. It's not until they meet their family members, often for the first time, that they begin to see the resemblance.

Only after we are introduced to the Holy Spirit, the One who created and formed us, can we understand who we really are. Immediately, we begin to see why we're on the Earth. The Holy Spirit gives us immediate access to our Dad, our Heavenly Father. When we see what He looks like, we can begin to understand why we look the way we do. We can then begin to access our true nature, our true self, our spirit. "God is a Spirit", [5]and so are we. He is the only Person who can reveal the missing pieces to our lives, revealing our true worth and value.

We are eternal supernatural beings having a very temporary natural experience.

5 John 4:24

THOUGHTS FOR TODAY:

☑ Self-awareness is the gateway to breakthrough.

☑ God designed my features to be in accordance with His plans for me.

☑ Each of these three areas within me: my spirit, soul and body... function uniquely, and have distinct needs.

☑ My spirit is my innermost being, the place where God connects and speaks to me.

☑ I need a renewed mind in order to know the will of God for my life.

☑ Only God can show me my missing pieces, revealing my true worth and value.

☑ I am an eternal supernatural being having a very temporary natural experience.

Add Five Minutes to Your Study

LEAN INTO LOVE

> "For we have the living Word of God, which is full of energy, and it pierces more sharply than a two-edged sword. It will even penetrate to the very core of our being where soul and spirit, bone and marrow meet! It interprets and reveals the true thoughts and secret motives of our hearts." - Hebrews 4:12 (TPT)

Think about this, the Word of God goes to the deepest places of your being. It penetrates the very core of who you are. It goes past the outer layers: your body, will, and emotions. It cuts right to your spirit, the person you were created to be. It reveals the exact thoughts and the secrets of your heart.

The Word of God is so powerful, it can bring clarity instantly in the core of our being.

TAKE THE LEAP

Take a moment to talk to God in prayer today. Ask Him to forgive you for speaking so hatefully about yourself. Ask Him to give you fresh eyes to see who He created you to be. Ask Him to help you see your tendency to spiral into a self-loathing commentary. Ask Him to change your perspective and begin to thank Him for the way He created you.

You don't always have to feel something right away for it to work. But as you speak it out, agreeing with the truth about who you are, you will begin to change. *Transformation is a journey, not a destination.* Keep going!

What did God say to me today?

Day Eight
MY TRUE SELF VS. PERSONALITY

> "Beauty isn't about having a pretty face. It's about having a pretty mind, a pretty heart, and most importantly a beautiful soul." - T.D. Jakes

I'm an identical twin. A mirror twin. 10% of identical twins are mirror twins. The reason they're called mirror twins is that it's like looking into a mirror. I'm left-handed, my sister is right-handed. We are very similar. (Honestly, she's the prettiest person I've ever met. I'm sorry ... twin joke. Ha!)

Most of my twin friends are going to understand this when I say that being a twin is all about comparison. Growing up as a twin, you always hear things like, "Now get together and let's see who is taller" or, "Who's the one with the round face and who's the one with the skinny face?" I understood... people were just trying to learn the difference between the two of us. Also, I think seeing someone who looks exactly like someone else is one of the more mysterious things in life.

It wasn't just our outside that was compared. From an early age, I remember my mom and dad calling me the lion and my sister Deborah was called the lamb. I distinctly remember them saying during my childhood, "Havilah will do it! She's a lion." I didn't mind being called the lion. I often felt excited that my parents defined us differently. I grew up thinking I was aggressive, outgoing, brave and super social. And that was okay because, after all, I was seemingly confident.

As I grew into adulthood, eventually marrying and living with Ben, I was in a different environment for the first time. Almost immediately the change encouraged characteristics and qualities I had never seen before in myself. I wasn't as aggressive as I thought I was, or opinionated. I wasn't the driver in the relationship. I was more joyful than driven, adventurous than aggressive. I was a homebody more than a socialite. I didn't change completely; I just showed up different in various situations.

As this awareness began to emerge in my life, I began to question my jerk reactions to life. I would stop to ask myself, "Do I really want to go to that party?" or "Is that something that's really me or just something I expect from myself?" I began reevaluating my thoughts.

It's important to understand that the environment we grew up in also dictated negative behavior in us. These behaviors were often a protective layer to help us survive.

Do you remember what we talked about on day three? How growing up as babies, we were born with a wide range of emotions? Our caregiver could intentionally or unintentionally suppress specific emotions in us when they didn't feel prepared or willing to deal with them. This is vital to understand. There are parts of us that were formed early on to protect us in our environments. Specifically, to help us deal with the pain of our childhood. These protective layers helped develop our personalities. Your personality kept you functioning in the environment of your development.

"Our personalities draw upon the capacities of our inborn temperament to develop defenses and compensations for where we

have been hurt in childhood. In order to survive whatever difficulties we encountered at the time, we unwittingly mastered a limited repertoire of strategies, self-images, and behaviors that allowed us to cope with and survive In our environment." [6]

These strategies were developed to fulfill our role in our family units.

Think about it for a second. What role did you have in your home growing up?

Here are a few ideas to get you started:

⌘ *The Scapegoat* - taking the blame to divert attention from other severe problems.

⌘ *The Baby* - dependence, weakness, vulnerability, need for protection, immaturity, greediness, and insatiability.

⌘ *The Pet* - showered with love, attention, and praise, even when undeserved.

⌘ *The Peacemaker* - assumed the role of an adult prematurely; to suppress the anxieties and concerns appropriate to the situation and his/her age.

These images and behaviors helped shape our personality.

Think about the life of Joseph in the Bible for a moment.

"Israel loved Joseph more than any of his other sons because he was the child of his old age. And he made him an elaborately embroidered coat. When his brothers realized that their father loved him more than them, they grew to hate him—they wouldn't even speak to him." - Genesis 37:3-4 (MSG)

6 The Wisdom of the by Donna Richard Rizzo and Russ Hudson Page 28

Joseph's dad favored him, which severely affected his relationships with his brothers. Eventually escalating it to the point where his brothers would fake Joseph's death and sell him to foreigners. I wonder how different Joseph's life would have been if his dad hadn't favored him? His Dad had a role for Joseph before he could understand the danger and pain it would bring to his life.

When our personality becomes the source of our identity, we lose contact with our spirit and deep connection to God. When we lose touch with our inner being, the one we were created to be, we can experience deep anxiety. This anxiety begins to drive our lives unconsciously or consciously.

When we connect with the person God created us to be, the work of transformation begins. We are no longer living up to someone else's expectation or even our own. We start to settle into our divine architecture. It takes maturity, wisdom, humility, and a whole lot of Holy Spirit to admit we've propped up an identity on anything other than God Himself.

It is a process and took me a long time to understand this. I know living in a safe protective home is extremely valuable. But, on the other hand, we can be sheltered from so much of our protective layers — the ones we've used to keep us safe from the outside world. We can have very good parents who do their very best, but they have limitations, too.

God is the ultimate Parent. Only He knows our full potential. When we agree with His potential, and not just what other people think our potential may be, we begin to see the miraculous operating in our own lives.

So, the goal is not to try to clean up our personalities by making sure we think the right thoughts, say the right words, or do the right things. It's about getting connected to God in a way that reveals the real person He created. The only way we can begin to grow from the inside out is to connect with our Source (God Himself). He is the only One who can change us.

When we are busy performing for the picture in our head, we know deep down that we are not entirely authentic. I don't mean that anytime we don't want to do something or something feels out of character; we slap on a sticker that says "That's not me!" It just means that God wants to show us that even in the face of struggle and difficulty we can begin to live with an inner peace. We can know we are who He created us to be, living contented, nothing more and nothing less. Remember, we want to live fully present to our purpose on the planet.

So today we're going to do a little soul work.

First, let me ask you a question. What was your role in your family growing up?

It could be something undeniable or maybe something you've never really thought about before. Were you the caretaker, the giver, the problem solver, the screw up, the pseudo-spouse, the spiritual one, etc.?

WRITE DOWN ONE OR TWO ROLES YOU FILLED IN YOUR HOME BELOW.

_____

_____

_____

NOW, TAKE A MOMENT AND TRY TO REMEMBER A MOMENT WHILE GROWING UP WHERE THIS ROLE WAS EXPECTED.

_____

_____

_____

_____

WAS THERE A TIME WHEN YOU RESISTED THE ROLE AND TRIED TO BREAK OUT OF THE MOLD, ONLY TO BE PUSHED RIGHT BACK INTO IT?

_____

_____

_____

_____

After you've acknowledged these moments and roles in your childhood, I want you to ask God who He created you to be. Write down what you hear Him saying about you.

I remember a time in my life when I felt as if every phone call I received involved solving a problem a friend or relative was having. After starting Christian counseling, I realized that many of these issues were their responsibility and not mine. In truth, they weren't doing anything out of the ordinary; they were merely asking me to do what I had done all along. Fulfill my role. Live from my personality. Solve the issue.

As I dug deeper into my spirit, I saw I was the problem solver in their lives. I was living with a savior mentality. My pay off was that I felt needed and wanted but the consequence was carrying burdens I wasn't intended to bear. It left me feeling tired all the time, burned out and depleted. It wasn't God's best for my life. He wanted to be their Savior, so I needed to step out of the way for this to happen.

After asking God who He created me to be, I found it was to bring gratitude and joy into every environment. So, I realized my personality was the scapegoat I used to feel needed. But, my inner being, the spirit man that God created me to be, was designed to bring His presence, joy, and gratitude into every environment. And I knew the only way this could happen was to be in touch with Him and know my purpose. I didn't have to perform for anyone. This sets us free. The pressure is off.

I heard Him call me at one point His Joy Girl, and that's what I chose to be. It took many years of deconstructing the parts of me that only felt worthy because of the role I played. But I want you to know something. The more connected we are to who God says we are, the more authentic we feel.

TRUTH: The more we perform for others, the more we deceive ourselves. In the end, we become mere reflections of who we believe others want us to be.

So, in humility, take some time to ask the Holy Spirit to reveal the hidden parts within your personality. Ask Him to do the work that only He can do by revealing the authentic person He created you to be.

THOUGHTS FOR TODAY:

- ☑ The environments I grew up in often dictate certain behaviors in me.

- ☑ My caregiver could intentionally or unintentionally block specific emotions from me when they didn't feel prepared to deal with them.

- ☑ Protective layers helped me deal with the pain of childhood, forming my personality. My personality kept me functioning in the environment of my development.

- ☑ When my personality becomes the source of my identity, I lose contact with my spirit and a deep connection with God.

- ☑ When I connect with the person God created me to be, the work of transformation begins.

- ☑ When I am busy performing for the picture in my head, I know deep down that I am not entirely authentic.

- ☑ The more I perform for others, the more I don't belong to myself; I belong to their picture of me.

Add Five Minutes to Your Study

 LEAN INTO LOVE

> "Don't, enemy, crow over me. I'm down, but I'm not out. I'm sitting in the dark right now, but God is my light. I can take God's punishing rage. I deserve it — I sinned. But it's not forever. He's on my side and is going to get me out of this. He'll turn on the lights and show me his ways. I'll see the whole picture and how right he is." - Micah 7:8-10 (MSG)

This passage is loaded with hope. I want us to focus on a few of these words today.

I'm down, but I'm not out.

I'm sitting in the dark right now, but God is my light.

He's on my side and is going to get me out of this.

Remember, you don't have to do anything on your own anymore. You have an Advocate (John 14:16) Whose only purpose is to help you. WOW! Think about that for a moment. Breathe it in!

He'll turn on the lights and show me His ways.

I'll see the whole picture and how right He is.

The Holy Spirit can't wait to turn all the lights on in your spirit and show you the real picture of who you are. Remember, living only by your personality creates anxiety. Well, the opposite is also true. When we live from our spirit, we have an indescribable peace. A peace that allows us to be fully present to our purpose on the planet.

TAKE THE LEAP

Take a moment to find a picture of yourself at a young age (around 6 or 7 years of age.)

 Ask yourself some questions:

What was I like at this age? What fears did I have? What hopes did I have?

Begin to see the innocence and authenticity you once had.

Ask the Holy Spirit to give you more of a childlike heart when you deal with yourself. I like to use the phrase, "Be nice to the little girl or boy inside of you." Why? Because that's how God sees and treats us, with kindness and compassion.

Day Nine
MY UNCHANGEABLE FEATURES

> "Sometimes I feel my whole life has been one big rejection." -Marilyn Monroe

The funny thing is she picked them up at a yard sale for next to nothing, and had them reupholstered with the fabric she wanted. I would never have picked up those chairs, much less had them repurposed. But she looked past their tattered condition, and saw the potential beauty in them. Now, we're all really grateful. I'm hoping to inherit them ... but don't tell my sister. :)

Today, let's reconsider your way of thinking. Perhaps you'll see what you've never seen before. In fact, you may have resigned these thoughts to a barren garage in your heart. But, it may become something you revisit time and again. It may even become one of your favorite thoughts about yourself.

I want us to reframe some of the ways we've been thinking about ourselves. Like, our outside: our bodies, bone structure, hair, eyes, skin color, curves or lack of curves, ethnicity, background, heritage, and lineage. Some of these dimensions we may be ashamed of, and some of these things we may consider our "best features." But they are the unchangeable features God chose for us to have on the planet.

YOUR FEATURES

Consider this. Before you were born, God designed your features in accordance with His plans for your life.

Have you ever thought of this before?

Your outside form is important to God as well.

Let's look at some things together:

Job writes:

"You made me like a handcrafted piece of pottery—
... Don't you remember how beautifully you worked my clay?" Job
10:8-9 (MSG)

Job is aware that God didn't just throw him together. He was unique and handcrafted. What makes pottery so unique? No two are alike. God doesn't create molds. He handcrafts each of us and forms us to fit His perfect plan. God loves originals! Think about it. No two snowflakes, pieces of sand, specks of dust, are the same. God loves to create, it's in His nature. He never runs out of originality. He loves to display Himself in His creation.

And again in the beauty of the Psalms we read,

"Oh yes, you shaped me first inside, then out; you formed me in my mother's womb. I thank you, High God—you're breathtaking! Body and soul, I am marvelously made! I worship in adoration—what a creation! You know me inside and out, you know every bone in my body; You know exactly how I was made, bit by bit, how I was sculpted from nothing into something. Like an open book, you watched me grow from conception to birth; all the stages of my life were spread out before you, the days of my life all prepared before I'd even lived one day." - Psalm 139:16 (MSG)

The Psalmist reminds us that God formed us before we ever entered our mother's womb. He watched every bone form, each part was tailor-made, crafted to perfection. Created on purpose, to look a specific way for a very important purpose.

Why is this important for us to understand? Because learning to embrace our whole self: body, soul, and spirit, is the foundation of self-acceptance. God doesn't want us to love our heart while divorcing our bodies. We can't fully embrace who we were created to be without embracing all of us, even the things we don't find beautiful.

"If what you see in the mirror is an example of God's passion and creativity, but you HATE it, how can you really trust Him for your life? You are an example of his most significant work." [7]

The more we learn to accept our bodies, the more we can accept the will of God for our lives. Actually, our obsession with our bodies takes on a new perspective when we are in tune with God and his purpose.The more we can trust God's motives in making us the way we are was all good. It will take us going deep in order to see there is a plan in all of it.

 There is a story of a Christian woman named Madam Guyon in the 17th century who was very wealthy and beautiful. But because she felt her beauty distracted her from knowing the Lord, she prayed that He would take her beauty away. She developed smallpox and ended up with scars all over her face. When she was given a mirror, she smiled and said, "Thank you, God." I know this sounds extreme but you get the point. It was her desire to love God with all her heart and she didn't want anything to get in the way.

In the same way, God doesn't want us so enamored with our bodies that we forget to cultivate the inner qualities that will last for eternity. If your confidence is only in how you look, you will

7 Institute of Basic Youth Conflicts

be left in fear that when your beauty fades, so will your worth. We will each have to work hard to not buy into the lie that we're more valuable because of how we look. Beauty is in the eye of the beholder. God loves the way we look because He created us to look like this. No matter what the world defines as beautiful, it will never measure up to how God defines beauty.

DISTORTED ABSOLUTES

Why do we often have a hard time embracing our bodies? Because from the very beginning, our enemy wanted us to believe we were made wrong. He's worked very hard trying to get us to buy into the lie that there is only good and bad, ugly and beautiful when it comes to creation. God is either good or bad, kind or evil, and we are either good or bad, beautiful or ugly. The devil lives in these distorted absolutes.

One lie Satan heavily relies upon when it comes to distorting our beauty is getting us to believe we are short changed.. **He's hoping we will be convinced that there is only one defined UNIVERSAL BEAUTY.** Everything else will never measure up. Sure, it may be pretty in its own way but it's not the ultimate vision of perfection. If he can get us to believe that beauty only looks one way, we will quickly dismiss and miss the true value around us: specifically the excellence and beauty we each possess.

A Universal <s>que</s> Beauty

··· There's only one ME.

Remember, **your purpose isn't to be beautiful.** I know that sounds funny, but if you listen to the world's messaging, beauty is at the top of the shortlist for 'must haves.' Plastic surgery is at its all time high. Everyone is trying to change their outward to satisfy the inward. As a follower of Christ, we can be beautiful, but our purpose is to emulate the image of Christ on the Earth, not the Kardashians. When we chase beauty, we lose the true essence of our purpose. We buy into the lie that our value is only skin deep. We mask the pain inside.

Can we be beautiful and emulate the image of Christ? Absolutely! But, if we have to choose one, we should be chasing the only fulfilling option: to live bigger on the inside than on the outside. To be beautiful from the inside out! Haven't you met people who are not necessarily attractive on the outside but radiate beauty? There is something about a person who is content and comfortable.

"For those whom He foreknew [of whom He was aware and loved beforehand], He also destined from the beginning [foreordaining them] to be molded into the image of His Son [and share inwardly His likeness], that He might become the firstborn among many brethren." - Romans 8:29 (AMPC)

When we try and copy an earthly image, it loses its dynamism. Originality captures the world's eyes. The more we discover our own beauty and live out our full potential, we are agreeing with God. Self Acceptance is learning to agree with God about yourself.

THOUGHTS FOR TODAY:

- ☑ I have unchangeable features God chose for me to have on the planet.

- ☑ God designated my features in accordance with His plans for my life.

- ☑ My outside form is, likewise, important to God.

- ☑ Every part of me was created on purpose, to look a specific way and for a very important purpose.

- ☑ If my confidence is only in how I look, I will be left in fear that when my beauty fades, so will my worth.

☑ My enemy is hoping I will believe there is only one defined Universal Beauty.

☑ My purpose isn't to be beautiful; my purpose is to emulate the image of Christ on the planet.

☑ Self Acceptance is learning to agree with God about myself.

Add Five Minutes to Your Study

 LEAN INTO LOVE

> "But doom to you who fight your Maker— you're a pot at odds with the potter! Does clay talk back to the potter: 'What are you doing? What clumsy fingers!'
> Isaiah 45:9-10 (MSG)

Stop to think about how many times you talk down about yourself, specifically about your body. We are a nation obsessed with the outward. It could be as simple as, "My legs are too fat." or even stronger, "I hate what I look like." It's normal for us to struggle with some part of our physical body, but I want you to repurpose this idea (Yep, like my Mom's chairs.) Think about God standing with you as you look in the mirror. He's wearing an apron. Clay covers His hands and the front of His apron. It looks as if He just got done sculpting something. That something is you! Think about looking at Him in the eye and saying, "I hate the way I look! Did you even try? You are so clumsy, God!" Sadly, this may be exactly what we are doing though we may never have thought about it like this.

Take a moment to read and meditate on Psalms 139. Consider highlighting or journaling the words that stand out to you.

 TAKE THE LEAP

Take a moment to talk to God in prayer. Ask God to forgive you for speaking so hatefully about the way you were made. Ask Him to give you fresh eyes to see your form and the way He created you. Ask Him to remind you when you start to spiral into a self-loathing commentary. Choose to thank Him for the way He created you. We don't always have to feel something right away in order for it to work. But as we speak it out, agreeing with truth, we will begin to change. Transformation is a journey, not a destination. Keep going!

Day Ten
REFLECTION DAY

RECORD: WHAT HAPPENED THIS WEEK FOR YOU?

_____

_____

_____

_____

_____

WHAT WAS YOUR PREVAILING EMOTION?

_____

_____

_____

_____

_____

_____

THOUGHT: WHAT DID YOU LEARN ABOUT YOURSELF

_____

_____

_____

_____

SKETCH: HOW WOULD YOU DRAW IT?

REFLECT: WHAT ARE YOU INVITING INTO YOUR LIFE WITH YOUR ACTIONS?

_____

_____

_____

_____

_____

CONCLUSION: IN ONE SENTENCE, WRITE YOUR MOST PROVOKING THOUGHT THAT WOULD MOVE YOU FORWARD:

_____

_____

_____

_____

_____

_____

THE PROCESS
BUILDING CONFIDENCE
Week Three

A few years ago, while I was speaking in Nashville, Ben and Judah flew in to join me so we could celebrate Judah's 10th birthday. I had meetings the day before, so the next day we'd planned to give Judah the whole day to do whatever He wanted to do. If you've been to Nashville, you know it's a stunning city. The southern town is full of so many beautiful places to visit — places like cozy coffee shops, old city music halls, and historical museums.

Judah wanted nothing to do with any of these things. First on his list? Find the nearest Lego store! And that's what we did. Loading up our luggage, popping into our four-door rental car, and driving toward the nearest Lego store.

You could see the enjoyment in Judah's face as we entered the store. He roamed around like a pinball, trying to take it all in. "Mom, look at this," and "Oh, I want this next time." There's nothing like having a front row to your kid's experience of something they love.

Eventually, the store clerk walked up to us, asking if we'd seen the new featured screen in the back. Not having seen it, we trailed behind her as she led us towards the back of the store. Walking toward the screen, we could see ourselves on film as the screen mirrored our movements.

She continued, "Watch this!" and grabbed one of the boxes of legos and held it in front of the screen. After a few seconds, you could also see a 3-D rendition of the project, the one the box would create, illuminating on top of the box. So if there was a bridge inside, you could see the bridge in a 3-D form sitting on top of the box she was holding.

It was incredible! We quickly grabbed a box to see if it would work for us. Here's the Statue of Liberty! Here's a pirate ship. We were fully engaged! Eventually, I sat back and watched Ben and Judah continue in excitement.

As I was standing there, right smack dab in the middle of the Lego store, I heard the Lord whisper to me, "That's what I want to do with you." I wanted to tease God, saying, "Do you mean - giving me a bunch of lego pieces and watching me struggle trying to put them all together?" I smiled at the thought.

But I knew He was getting to a more profound point. He said, "Your life can feel messy, like tons of pieces that need to fit together to make it work. It can feel overwhelming when you know it's all supposed to fit together, but you don't know how or what you are building. But this is what I want to do for you. I want to illuminate the picture of what you're building. I want to give you the bigger picture!" I knew He was right. It wasn't hard for me to think about the moments in my life where I didn't know how something would fit together but, as He gently helped me, as peace flooded my mind, my heart, and my emotions towards my purpose, I could begin to see what He was building.

I think Christians get this wrong a lot. We often ignore the work of understanding the way we were created, in hopes that our spirituality will fill in the blanks. And of course, Jesus fills in all the blanks, but if we don't understand the way in which we were created, we'll never be able to sustain a vibrant life.

So this week, we're taking your life and showing you what it looks like in front of God's big-screen. We're going to unpack how the pieces fit together so you can feel confident you're building the right way. Towards the end of the week, I'm going to show you how to remove the broken and displaced pieces in your lives. This week is all about the PLAN.

So, stick with me! Grab your Bible, a good cup of coffee, and an open heart. Let's get started!

Day Eleven
ATTACHING NEW MEANING

> "I hope one day your human body is not a jail cell; instead, it's a sunny garden with daisies thriving because of self-love."
> - Anonymous

I was in my house working one day with a daytime talk show on in the background. I hadn't noticed the topic until one of the guests on the show asked what the psychologist they were interviewing thought of plastic surgery and altering our appearance. It quickly grabbed my attention. I was curious how this man would navigate such a hot American topic. The guest began to share her story.

"I've been on the cover of every magazine in the world," said the supermodel. "But as a young model, I never felt as beautiful as I looked. I masked it well with alcoholism. I grew up in an abusive home and was told on a daily basis by my father that I would never amount to anything and that I looked like a boy. One of the main reasons I had a lot of plastic surgery was because of the voice of my father.... I'm addicted to cosmetic surgery! But plastic surgery hasn't stifled the voice from my father."

I sat back in my seat, taking in what I had just witnessed. My story is nothing like this woman, so why would her words so profoundly resonate with me? Why was there an immediate hush over the room the moment she said this? I think deep down I've been caught believing the lie she believed herself.

If I could just change that one thing on my body, I'd lose the feeling of shame and live more confidently.

It shows up in phrases I've used like; "If I could lose a little more weight, I'd finally like my body." or "If I could stop my cystic acne, I'd finally like one picture of myself." Like a carrot on a string, just one more change was needed and it would affirm the value of my life. I know I'd feel more confident in who I am.

But that's never where it stops. Hate always grows and robs us of love. I've known what it's like to look in the mirror and not be able to find one thing I liked about the way I looked. Welcome to my teen years! At times, I've told my body, "I hate you. I hate the way you make me feel. I hate that you look nothing like the person I feel on the inside."

Every one of us has a child inside, and this child has a voice. Clearly, the voice of this woman's father haunted her. It didn't matter what the world thought of her, or how stunningly beautiful she may have been. The voice of rejection was the dominating force in her life. I think each of us can think of a moment, or maybe many moments, in our lives where a negative narrative about our appearance scarred us. It doesn't matter if what someone said was true or not, they just needed us to believe it.

Rejection comes at different points in each of our lives. It's not a matter of 'IF' rejection will come, but 'WHEN'. We live in a fallen world where hurt people, hurt people. Often the rejection we face comes from the outside. Like the woman above, we have been mocked, ridiculed, and bullied about our physical appearance. Those hurtful words have, in some way, defined how we see ourselves and even the value of our physical bodies.

I once had a friend tell me this story. She was with a friend at a beach and they were both wearing bathing suits. She asked her friend timidly, "Ok, be totally honest with me. Do you think I could take my shorts off, or are my thighs too big? Can I get away with not wearing shorts?" Her friend bluntly replied, "You should wear shorts." She said from that moment on she never wore a bathing suit without shorts again, and this was 15 years later. The words of her friend altered her life. I wonder how many of us hide, cover up, and live ashamed of parts of our physical body because of someone else's words.

But there's also a different type of rejection many of us face. It's the rejection of the way we were created on the outside. Often, this is due to a physical defect like a birthmark, disability, deformity, or a physical characteristic that's uncommon or even abnormal. A negative defining feature.

It leaves us feeling that **my body is a burden.**

These physical features can cause us to ask the question, "Why would a loving, all-powerful Creator God allow imperfections like these to exist?"

My Body is A burden. BEAUTY.

I want to remind us the world is broken. When Adam and Eve ate the fruit of the forbidden tree, it allowed brokenness to enter our world. The Bible says that all creation groans for things to be right again,

"For against its will the universe itself has had to endure the empty futility resulting from the consequences of human sin. But now, with eager expectation, all creation longs for freedom from its slavery to decay and to experience with us the wonderful freedom coming to God's children. To this day we are aware of the universal agony and groaning of creation, as if it were in the contractions of labor for childbirth." - Romans 8:20-23 (TPT)

Some of our defects are caused by the brokenness of another person. Maybe in the womb, their irresponsibility has affected the way you were born. Maybe an accident happened due to someone's negligence and it's affected your physical body. Other times we are just born with the defect with no apparent reason why.

So, how do we process the parts of our life that are imperfect? How do we help those closest to us understand God's plan in the pain, the defect, the deficiency?

In the Old Testament, a child named Mephibosheth was dropped and became disabled in both of his feet. (2 Samuel 4:4) This physical handicap caused Mephibosheth to refer to himself as a "dead dog." (2 Samuel 9:8) Only the kindness of King David allowed him to live a content life. (2 Samuel 19:30)

In the New Testament, the paraphrased words of Paul the Apostle offer some insight.

"The physical part of you is not some piece of property belonging to the spiritual part of you. God owns the whole works. So let people see God in and through your body." - 1 Corinthians 6:19-20 (MSG)

Every human being has been touched by the effects of sin. We all have defects whether they are mental, physical, spiritual, or emotional. In the face of these harsh realities, God mercifully works to redeem each of our painful experiences.

Romans reminds us:
"So we are convinced that every detail of our lives is continually woven together to fit into God's perfect plan of bringing good into our lives, for we are his lovers who have been called to fulfill his designed purpose." - Romans 8:28 (TPT)

What Romans is telling us is that we can actually live convinced that every detail of our lives, even our defects, can be woven together to fit into God's perfect plan. Remember, God's desire is to bring His goodness into everyone's life, which would fulfill one purpose of making Him known.

The Church is really good about communicating messages that the inside of us matters. And it does! But, accepting our spirit and soul on the inside can never be fully realized without accepting of our bodies on the outside. God wants to provide a way for us to view our physical frame with His spiritual eyes in order for us to accept, enhance, and enjoy how He made us.

"The body plays a critical role in all forms of genuine spiritual work, because bringing awareness back to the body anchors the quality of Presence. The reason is fairly obvious: While our minds and feelings can wander into the past or the future, our bodies can only exist here and now, in the present moment. This is one of the fundamental reasons why virtually all meaningful spiritual work begins with coming back to the body and becoming more grounded in it."[8]

Here are a few ways we can **Attach New Meaning to Our Flaws.**

1. We can define our flaws as **Marks of Ownership.**

"...who has placed his mark of ownership upon us, and who has given us the Holy Spirit in our hearts as the guarantee of all that he has in store for us." - 2 Corinthians 1:22 (GNT)

Redefining our flaws as marks of ownership can consistently remind us of Whom we belong to. We can use our body, our flaws, to bring glory to God.

8 The wisdom of the Enneagram by Don Richard Riso and Russ Hudson. (Page 51)

It reminds me of a story I heard growing up. There was a boy who was born with a large birthmark on his face. His Dad made it his mission to affirm the mark by telling the little boy God had marked him because he belonged to Him. The dad never stopped reminding the boy of this as he grew. One day, when the boy was older, he came to his dad with a serious look. *"Dad, you know the mark on my face, the one that tells me God loves me and I belong to Him? Well, I kind of feel bad for all the other kids who don't have a mark like mine."*

His dad's ability to define this little boy's birthmark as a mark of ownership helped shape the son's heart, and it also brought glory to God. It wasn't a burden for him to bear, but rather a mark of blessing for him to adore. I wonder how our lives would change if we stopped looking at our flaws as burdens and began seeing them as blessings and marks of ownership? If we look closely, we may see God's fingerprints over all humanity.

2. Our flaws can motivate us to **Develop Inward Qualities.**

There is no such thing as the 'ideal *outward* beauty' but God is definitely clear on the 'ideal *inward* beauty.' What does inward beauty look like? Actually, we should be asking the question, *"Who are we trying to emulate?"*

"For he knew all about us before we were born and he destined us from the beginning to share the likeness of his Son. This means the Son is the oldest among a vast family of brothers and sisters who will become just like him." - Romans 8:29 (TPT)

Our happiness isn't dependant on an outward beauty, which only lasts for a short time on Earth. But our happiness will always be connected to our ability to experience the eternal character of Jesus being formed in our lives. As branches, we only grow lasting fruit when we have the fruit of the Spirit in our lives.

"But the fruit produced by the Holy Spirit within you is divine love in all its varied expressions: joy that overflows, peace that subdues, patience that endures, kindness in action, a life full of virtue, faith that prevails, gentleness of heart, and strength of spirit. Never set the law above these qualities, for they are meant to be limitless." - Galatians 5:22-23 (TPT)

3. Our flaws can inspire us to **Serve Others Well.**

If you want to be great, learn to be a servant.

If you want to be known

If you want to be present, learn to listen.

And if you want to have purpose, learn to see your life from God's perspective.

BE known for Serving Others

"You are to lead by a different model. If you want to be the greatest one, then live as one called to serve others." - Mark 10:43 (TPT)

Most people have some physical, mental, emotional, or family flaw. If you have experienced rejection from others and yet learned to see your life from God's perspective by accepting God's design for yourself, you should be highly motivated to serve others, by listening to them—especially those with obvious flaws.

THOUGHTS FOR TODAY:

- ☑ God designated my features in accordance with His plans for my life.

- ☑ It's not a matter of 'IF' rejection will come, but 'WHEN' rejection will come.

- ☑ God mercifully works to redeem every painful circumstance in my life.

- ☑ Live convinced that every detail of my life, even my flaws, can be woven together to fit into God's perfect plan.

- ☑ Redefining my flaws as marks of ownership can consistently remind me of Whom I belong to.

- ☑ There is no 'ideal outward beauty'; only an 'ideal inward beauty' seen by God alone.

- ☑ My happiness will always be connected to my ability to experience the character of Jesus being developed in my life.

- ☑ If I want to be great, learn to be a servant.

Add Five Minutes to Your Study

 ### LEAN INTO LOVE

> "You were God's expensive purchase, paid for with tears of blood, so by all means, then, use your body to bring glory to God!" - 1 Corinthians 6:20 (TPT)

How valuable are you? You are so valuable to God, He would have sent His only Son, Jesus Christ, to die in your place, even if you were the only one who needed redemption. You are so valuable to God, He gave His life to rescue you!

 ### TAKE THE LEAP

Take a moment to write down every fruit of the Spirit (Galatians 5:22-23) you could allow to grow in your life. Circle the top two you would love to see increase in your life this year. Ask the Holy Spirit to help you increase the evidence of His power working in and through your life.

Write your thoughts here...

Day Twelve
AWARENESS + AWAKENING

> "You have to be brave with your life so that others can be brave with theirs." - Katherine Center

A pastor friend of my Dad lived in the Yukon Territory, one of the northern-most provinces of Canada. One winter day, he went on snowmobiles with a couple of natives. Hours into their journey a violent storm came upon them. After a long period of fighting the snow, their lead guide gestured for the three of them to stop and talk. With howling winds and piercing snow buffeting them, they huddled together. The guide confessed, "I think we're lost. I've grown up here my whole life, and I've never seen this rise in the terrain before." At those words, the pastor's heart sank. Their guide was renowned. For him to be lost in a blinding snowstorm was terrifying and unexpected. After a few moments of consideration, the pastor said, "We need to pray!" Bowing their heads in desperation, they asked the Lord for His mercy and guidance.

Following an emotional prayer, one of them spoke up, "I believe we've been going in the wrong direction. Because of the intensity of the storm, we've been going with the wind. What we need to do now is drive directly into the wind and snow."

For a few moments after this unorthodox declaration, they remained silent. Either this radical recommendation was a Word of Knowledge, or it would lead them to certain death.

After another desperate prayer, they decided to receive the counsel. Though the wind and snow continued to batter them, they drove directly into the storm and eventually made it safely home. Their lives had been spared.

What saved them?

In addition to the grace of God, they had been willing to do what hurt the most: *face their fears and drive directly into the unknown.*

Sometimes you have to walk through pain to get to pleasure.

I don't know about you, but the tension between *self-awareness and spiritual awakening* can often lead me to feel anxious. When I get a glimpse of freedom, and it's in an unknown area, I can quickly feel vulnerable to fear and anxiety. Thoughts like, *"What if I get stuck and don't know where I am"* or the *"I should have seen this before"* can leave me reactive, initially feeling worse than before I had them.

It's very similar to how we can feel after working out. Because some of us don't work out consistently (insert me raising my hand here), each time we hit the gym, we leave almost immediately feeling worse. **The truth is that even though we did something really good for ourselves, initially we often feel more pain than pleasure.**

I wonder how many of us would go through radical transformation if we were willing to face our fears and pushed through the unknown? I wonder how many of us refuse to change because we bought into the lie, *"I've always been this way?"* or *"I'm too old or tired, too busy, discouraged, or heartbroken?"*

I think If God were to speak to you right now he would probably say, *"Sweetheart, you're going to have to go through the pain and discomfort to get to the peace and freedom."*

Here's the truth: in order for any of us to grow spiritual muscles on the inside of us, we have to be willing to have them broken down. We have to push past the thoughts that say, *"This is uncomfortable and the pain is unbearable."*

"Although we might wish that spiritual growth would be more linear and that it could be accomplished in one or two major breakthroughs, the reality is that it is a process that we must go through many times on many different fronts until our whole psyche is reorganized."[9]

How do we push through to Spiritual Awakening?

It's taken each of us years to build up our soul defenses, resulting in our personalities. In order for us to live spiritually awakened, and sustain a spiritual path, we will need to work out our salvation. (Philippians 2:12)

What does this mean? God will lovingly point out an area where we have believed a lie about ourselves or about Him. We will be spiritually awakened to the truth! But at this moment we have a choice to make. The awakening alone will not sustain our transformation. We will need to partner with the Holy Spirit and live in the self-awareness He just revealed, surrendering to the process of transformation. When I say process, I mean it doesn't happen overnight.

Transformation will always be a journey, never a destination.

"The process of growth entails an ongoing cycling among letting go of old blockages, opening up to new possibilities in ourselves, and then encountering deeper levels of blockage."[10]

9, 10 The wisdom of the Enneagram by Don Richard Riso and Russ Hudson. (Page 45)

We only change when our willingness to accept God-allowed pain exceeds our fears. At times, we will all suffer a sharp painful disillusionment before we fully surrender.

"Though we experience every kind of pressure, we're not crushed. At times we don't know what to do, but quitting is not an option. We are persecuted by others, but God has not forsaken us. We may be knocked down, but not out. We continually share in the death of Jesus in our own bodies so that the resurrection life of Jesus will be revealed through our humanity." - 2 Corinthians 4:8-10 (TPT)

Spiritual growth is a process.

I want us to look at 2 Peter together.

"Everything we could ever need for life and complete devotion to God has already been deposited in us by his divine power. For all this was lavished upon us through the rich experience of knowing him who has called us by name and invited us to come to him through a glorious manifestation of his goodness." - 2 Peter 1:3 (TPT)

Once we accept Jesus as Lord of our lives and surrender to His leadership, the Bible says we are a new creation. (See 2 Corinthians 5:17) Our old man (old nature) has passed away but the new man (new nature) is being renewed day by day.

When our spirit is awakened, we have everything we need to live for God. The deepest parts of us are now alive. We now want to do what He wants us to do and we have the power to do it! So our struggles in life aren't because we didn't get everything God promised. The struggle comes from our old habits of sin, old mindsets, and our soulish personalities.

"Our soul has its own wisdom, and it will not allow us to see anything about ourselves (much less release it) until we are truly ready to do so."[11]

When we begin to see the promises God has given us and the access we have to them, we begin to let go of our soulish wisdom.

Continuing with 2 Peter...

"As a result of this, he has given you magnificent promises that are beyond all price, so that through the power of these tremendous promises you can experience partnership with the divine nature, by which you have escaped the corrupt desires that are of the world." - 2 Peter 1:4 (TPT)

Here is our communal purpose!

"So devote yourselves to lavishly supplementing your faith with goodness, and to goodness add understanding, and to understanding add the strength of self-control, and to self-control add patient endurance, and to patient endurance add godliness, and to godliness add mercy toward your brothers and sisters, and to mercy toward others add unending love." - 2 Peter 1:5-7 (TPT)

The good news is we already have these virtues resident in God's Spirit and available to each of us. They are planted deep within our spirit, and if yielded to, they will keep us from becoming fruitless in our pursuit of knowing Jesus Christ more intimately.

7 ESSENTIALS FOR SPIRITUAL GROWTH:

1. Read, learn and apply God's Word in your everyday life.

2. Allow the Word of God to teach, rebuke, correct, and train you.

11 The Wisdom of the Enneagram by Don Richard Riso and Russ Hudson. (Page 45)

3. Acknowledge habits of sin and actively resist them.

4. Choose to live from your spirit man and not your soulish lower nature.

5. Nurture a relationship with the Holy Spirit by letting Him lead and guide you.

6. Value Christ-like qualities by regularly focusing on and practicing them.

7. Purpose to grow in your faith and trust in God.

THOUGHTS FOR TODAY:

☑ When I get a glimpse of freedom, it's in an unknown area, so I can become vulnerable to fear and anxiety.

☑ In order for me to live a spiritually awakened life and sustain a spiritual path, I will need to work out my salvation. (Philippians 2:12)

☑ Transformation will always be a journey, never a destination.

☑ I only change when my willingness to accept God-allowed pain exceeds my fears.

☑ My struggle as a believer comes from my old habits of sin, old mindsets, and my soulish personality.

☑ When I begin to see all the promises God has given me and the access I have to them, I begin to let go of my soulish wisdom.

Add Five Minutes to Your Study

 LEAN INTO LOVE

> "Truth's shining light guides me in my choices and decisions;
> the revelation of your word makes my pathway clear."
> - Psalm 119:105 (TPT)

As we have talked about the seven essentials to spiritual growth, there's a lot to consider. Take a moment to think about which area you most need activated in your life? Write it down here:

_____

 TAKE THE LEAP

Take a moment to close your eyes right where you are. Quiet yourself. Ask the Holy Spirit to reveal one thing you can do today which would help you activate this essential area in your spiritual life. Write down what He tells you.

God spoke to my heart today...

_____

_____

_____

_____

_____

_____

_____

_____

_____

_____

_____

_____

_____

_____

_____

_____

_____

_____

SPIRIT-LED LIVING

> "I am the sprouting vine and you're my branches. As you live in union with me as your source, fruitfulness will stream from within you—but when you live separated from me you are powerless." - John 15:5 (TPT)

I was a 17-year-old church kid. In an effort to fit in at school and church, I spent the majority of my high school years trying to stay under the radar. One night, on the way to a party with my twin sister, Deborah, and a couple of guys, the Holy Spirit began to speak to me. His voice was strong and clear, "Havilah, you are called to more than this; you can't live like this. I have a call on your life!" Shocked. I felt compelled to speak out in the darkness. "Can you turn the music down?" I began, "I have a call on my life!" My words met with total silence. Now with tears streaming down my face, I continued. "You are welcome to come with me if you want, but this is what I'm going to do. I'm going to serve God." That night changed the trajectory of my whole life.

Your spirit is powerless unless it's connected to God. Jesus tells us, "You're my branches." Branches don't bear fruit unless they are connected to the vine.

I want to teach you a foundational truth you're going to need for the rest of your life. Take a moment to read through Genesis chapter one on your own.

There, we read that God created every living thing. He spoke it out and it was created.

✓ He spoke to the land to produce vegetation.

"Then God said, 'Let the land produce vegetation: seed-bearing plants and trees on the land that bear fruit with seed in it, according to their various kinds.' And it was so. The land produced vegetation: plants bearing seed according to their kinds and trees bearing fruit with seed in it according to their kinds. And God saw that it was good." - Genesis 1:11-12

✓ He spoke to the sky and placed the stars there.

"God made two great lights – the greater light to govern the day and the lesser light to govern the night. He also made the stars. God set them in the vault of the sky to give light on the earth, to govern the day and the night, and to separate light from darkness. And God saw that it was good." Genesis 1:16-18

✓ He spoke to the water. Creating separation from land and water for the fish.

"God spoke: 'Swarm, Ocean, with fish and all sea life! Birds, fly through the sky over Earth!' God created the huge whales, all the swarm of life in the waters..." - Genesis 1:23

✓ He created everything by speaking to the environment. But, when God created man, the Bible says He spoke to Himself.

"Then God said, 'Let us make mankind in our image, in our likeness, so that they may rule over the fish in the sea and the birds in the sky, over the livestock and all the wild animals, and over all the creatures that move along the ground.' So God created mankind in his own image, in the

image of God he created them; male and female he created them." - Genesis 1:26-27

HERE'S WHAT I WANT YOU TO SEE:

A *plant* has to stay connected to the *Earth* in order to live.

A *fish* has to stay in the *water* to live.

A *star* has to stay in *space* to fulfill its purpose.

A *man* has to stay connected to *God* to live and fulfill his purpose. We need a specific environment to live in.

You came out of God, so you need God in order to live. The Bible doesn't say we SHOULD be saved. It says we MUST be saved. (Acts 4:12) Jesus didn't say *"I am A way,"* He said *"I'm THE way."* The Bible isn't confused about our need for God. We shouldn't be either. The only way for us to reach our true potential is through Jesus.

We used to live in a town that was a twin city. Which meant, in order to access the other little town, we had to cross over a bridge. There wasn't any other way. Can you imagine if, one day, I didn't want to use that bridge any longer? In my frustration, I just sat on one side of the bridge refusing to cross over. What if I thought, *"I refuse to accept that this bridge is the only way for me to get to our twin city."* Would my adamancy in my belief change reality? Hardly! I'd merely be stuck believing unreality.

I realize this may seem like too simple of an analogy to explain salvation, but salvation wasn't meant to be for closed hearts, but open hearts; humble responses, not proud ones. The Bible encourages us to come to Jesus as little children. I like to think, *"If my kids don't understand what salvation is, then I'm making it too complex."*

Our need for Jesus is simple. He is the only Bridge to the Father, to eternity. Jesus is the Bridge to my full potential. My life source. My Dad always said, *"You may call God my crutch but you would be wrong. He's not my crutch; he's my feeding tube, my breathing machine. I can't live without Him."* You're not being needy to need God; it's the most authentic place you can live.

When we are spiritually dead, we are unaware of our full potential. We have no root system to keep us grounded in life. Jesus promised to reveal our true potential if we live connected to Him. But connected doesn't mean holding hands. It's like hanging onto a rope swing. Wherever He goes, I go. We are connected.

Satan's ultimate plan is to destroy the reality of who you are, and who God created you to be. Think about Adam and Eve for a minute. After they ate the fruit, everything changed.

Adam said, **'I heard the sound of You [walking] in the garden, and I was afraid because I was naked; so I hid myself.'" - Genesis 3:10 (AMP)**

Adam and Eve were naked and afraid. Why? Because when they ate the fruit their souls came alive! Remember, you are a spirit, but you possess a soul, that is housed in a body. Adam and Eve begin to immediately LIVE in their soul, not by their spirit. When they disobeyed God, their spirit became unplugged. When we don't come to God and let Him be Lord of our lives, we live unplugged. We live a soulish life. We then live only in a soulish realm.

When we live by the Spirit - we live from the *inside out.*

When we live by the soul - we live from the *outside in.*

Soulish living means we take what we want from the outside and try to put it on the inside of us. Spiritual living means we receive what we need from God on the inside and it grows to be visible on the outside. If you have no evidence of God's power and potential working in your life, it's guaranteed that you are not connected. You cannot bear good fruit without being connected to a healthy life source. A light bulb is worthless unless it's connected to electricity. Your spirit is powerless unless it is connected to God.

How do we stay connected to our source?

We have to *abide*.

We have to *remain*.

"Remain in Me, and I [will remain] in you. Just as no branch can bear fruit by itself without remaining in the vine, neither can you [bear fruit, producing evidence of your faith] unless you remain in Me." - John 5:4 (AMP)

Abide means to *stay in one place for a long time.* The root word for *remain* means to *stay through the struggle.* The longer you stay, the better the root system and the better the fruit.

Do you want to know an interesting fact?

The best grapes are the ones who have struggled.

ABIDE = Remain through the struggle

"Winemakers often want the vines to struggle a bit. A struggling plant will produce fewer grapes with a stronger flavor and more complexity, which produces high-quality wine." [12]

When we *remain*, we get really good fruit. We grow the kind of life that only comes after you've stuck with it for a while. In essence, we have to marry the Word: stay in relationship with it for a lifetime.

12 https://homeguides.sfgate.com/grapevine-root-systems-59167.html

I want to remind you, Jesus came to destroy the works of the devil.

"The reason the Son of God was revealed was to undo and destroy the works of the devil." - 1 John 3:8b (TPT)

Jesus came to destroy the works of the devil so we could have a full life in Him.

"...But I have come to give you everything in abundance, more than you expect—life in its fullness until you overflow!" - John 10:10 (TPT)

The root word for *abundant* is the word *fountain*. Jesus came to unleash (unlock) the fountain of your potential. Just like the words of Jesus in John,

"If anyone thirsts, let him come to me and drink. Rivers of living water will brim and spill out of the depths of anyone who believes in me this way, just as the Scripture says." - John 7:37-39 (MSG)

Jesus CAME to unleash your potential

God's rivers of living water become a fountain inside of you!

God doesn't show us our full potential immediately, because we need a root system strong enough to sustain it.

When we struggle, our struggle isn't with flesh and blood. It's with leadership in our life. When we are leading our own life, we only have access to a soulish way of life, a soulish way of thinking. When we struggle with fear, worry, shame, and unbelief, it means our soul man is leading. Faith, confidence, security, acceptance, and belonging means our spirit man is leading us.

THOUGHTS FOR TODAY:

- ☑ Until I am plugged into my source, I can't live authentic to whom I am created to be.

- ☑ The fruit is always in the root.

- ☑ Healthy things grow!

- ☑ When I begin living planted by God's design, connected to His spirit, I live a completely different life.

- ☑ I have an unlimited source of comfort, connection, and confidence coming from the inside of me.

- ☑ Without having Jesus as the center of my life, I will live disconnected and my life will deteriorate quickly.

Add Five Minutes to Your Study

 LEAN INTO LOVE

> Someone living on an entirely human level rejects the revelations of God's Spirit, for they make no sense to him. He can't understand the revelations of the Spirit because they are only discovered by the illumination of the Spirit.
> 1 Corinthians 2:14 (TPT)

Paul is telling us that only those who have an alive spirit can fully understand spiritual things. We can't judge a world for not being spiritual or understanding spiritual things, if they don't have the Holy Spirit (Our divine interpreter) on the inside of them.

Likewise, we can rest in knowing that our Spirit is alive to God. Whatever He wants us to hear or understand, He will help us. We have all the help we need, we just have to recieve it.

 TAKE THE LEAP

Take a moment today to acknowledge the Holy Spirit in your life. He is a person. He wants to have a relationship with you. Talk to Him, He's right there with you. Write Him a letter expressing your gratitude and love for Him.

> "A tree with a bitter root, can only produce bitter fruit."
> - Anonymous

A couple years ago we got a call from my parents. They asked if we could be on the phone with both of them because they had something they wanted to share with us. Anytime everyone is asked to be on the phone call in life, you kind of know it's either really good news or really bad news. Dad did all the talking. *"Well, guys, your mother and I wanted to share something with you. A couple of months ago your mother had a colonoscopy."* It was routine for her age, so she didn't let us know. My Dad continued, *"We just received the results back and it looks like your mom has some spots that the doctor is concerned about. He wants to go back in to take a biopsy and see if it's actually precancerous. Of course, we are concerned about this, but we thought we should let you know since this is beginning to escalate."*

Fast-forward a couple weeks later and they called again. This time you could hear a little more seriousness in their voices. *"Well, we got the news back from the doctor and it looks like some of the polyps have precancerous signs. The doctor wants to go back in and remove them and the tissue around the spots."* Of course, we were immediately concerned. Mom and Dad are at the age where you kind of begin to realize you don't have an unlimited amount of time with them on the Earth. So, for the next couple of weeks we were on high alert.

Another phone call. *"The doctor said the surgery went very well. He believes he got all of the spots as well as the tissue around them."* Now we were crying. Deeply relieved. Deeply grateful. *"Your mom will need to go in every year for a checkup to make sure it hasn't grown. We're so grateful for the skills of the doctor and the grace of God during this season."*

I know many of us have been touched by cancer. Whether it was a family member, a friend, or even ourselves. We all know that that word means life change. Because we know the seriousness of cancer, none of us are flippant about the topic. We understand that cancer can be fatal without intervention.

Just like physical cancer, we can also have cancer of the soul. It's the type of inner sickness, if not dealt with, that can eventually kill our spirit as well. And just like physical cancer, it needs an aggressive approach in order for us to stay spiritually alive.

"See to it that no one falls short of the grace of God and that no bitter root grows up to cause trouble and defile many. See that no one is sexually immoral, or is godless like Esau, who for a single meal sold his inheritance rights as the oldest son." - Hebrews 12:15-16 (NIV)

When someone becomes offended and doesn't deal with that offense the right way, it can grow into their soul and become a root of bitterness.

"The word "root" is the Greek word "ridzo". It refers to a root, such as the root of a tree. These are roots that have gone down deep and are now deeply embedded. Therefore, the word ridzo often denotes something that is established or firmly fixed.[1]

When the Bible uses the word *"ridzo"* it's telling us that bitterness doesn't just grow overnight. Bitterness always starts off with an offense (a sprout). An offense simply means an unresolved conflict with a loved one or friend. It hurts because it mattered to us. Over time, if we allow the unresolved conflict (the sprout) in our lives to build a case against the person, it eventually becomes a deeply embedded thought (a root) in the way we think about them.

"Once it becomes this deeply rooted in your soul, your negative opinion of the offender will become firmly fixed. As time passes, your thoughts of judgment against him will become more developed, rationalized, and established. That root of bitterness will become so firmly fixed inside you that your angry, judgmental thoughts about the person will actually begin to make sense to you."[14]

It reminds me of a friend who recently purchased a home. The home was a beautiful mountain home with oak trees around the property, sitting in the middle of five acres. The environment was pristine! When buying this home, however, they knew they needed to make some cosmetic changes. First thing on the list, expanding the kitchen into the small dining room. Should be simple since they didn't need to alter the square footage.

Really? No!

As they began the process, their contractor came back with some bad news. The foundation would not sustain the changes. The foundation had been compromised. They were blindsided.

They wanted to know exactly what had happened since the house wasn't very old. The contractor told them the roots of their beautiful oak trees had grown into the foundation, destroying its stability.

Gosh, isn't that a clear illustration? When we don't deal with the small things correctly, they have the potential of going deep into our foundation and shaking us to the core. Jesus said, *"Offenses will come."*[15] None of us are immune from dealing with conflict.

But the danger comes when we are not able to deal with conflict in a healthy way. If we allow the offense to stay in our lives, it will eventually seep into our root system and destroy our foundation.

"... becoming careless about God's blessings, like Esau who traded away his rights as the firstborn for a simple meal." - Hebrews 12:15-16 (TPT)

We each are vulnerable to the Esau Syndrome. Trading in a lifelong gift from God for a short-term appetite. Offense deceives us into believing our one meal of disobedience and bitterness is better than sitting at the table of forgiveness and abundance.

That's why the Apostle Paul warned, **"But I am afraid that just as Eve was deceived by the serpent's cunning, your minds may somehow be led astray from your sincere and pure devotion to Christ." - 2 Corinthians 11:3 (NIV)**

He's saying that he was afraid we would succumb to the original human sin.

Let's go back and look at this for a moment:

The serpent was clever, more clever than any wild animal God had made. He spoke to the Woman: "Do I understand that God told you not to eat from any tree in the garden?" The Woman said to the serpent, "Not at all. We can eat from the trees in the garden. It's only about the tree in the middle of the garden that God said, 'Don't eat from it; don't even touch it or you'll die.'" The serpent told the Woman, "You won't die. God knows that the moment you eat from that tree, you'll see what's really going on. You'll be just like God, knowing everything, ranging all the way from good to evil." Genesis 3:1-5 (MSG)

The serpent says, *"God knows..."* Which was the truth, but only a half-truth. Partial truth will always be the enemy's greatest weapon against us as believers. Deception always carries a little truth.

The Lie: God is holding out on you.

What is behind this lie? The original sin: a root of bitterness.

If the enemy of our soul can get us to believe that God isn't as good as He says He is, and if he can get us to question God's character, then everything else will fall apart.

God's whole Kingdom is built on truth. He is who He says He is, and He will do what He says He will do. Period.

God is a truth teller.

"God is not human, that he should lie, not a human being, that he should change his mind. Does he speak and then not act? Does he promise and not fulfill?" - Numbers 23:19 (NIV)

Surprisingly, Adam and Eve were not the first ones to sin.

The devil is the original sinner.

"The one who does what is sinful is of the devil, because the devil has been sinning from the beginning. The reason the Son of God appeared was to destroy the devil's work." - 1 John 3:8 (NIV)

The devil is trying to get Eve to question God's character. He wants to manipulate Eve into believing God deceived her. He wants her disappointment to grow into bitterness. *Why?* Because Satan is the author of all sin. His sin, the original sin, began with bitterness toward God. Satan, as an angel in heaven, believed God was holding out on him. (Isaiah 14) He allowed a root of bitterness towards God to form in him, eventually becoming his demise.

All sin is bitterness towards God and most of our deepest bitterness is directed toward God. It's connected to the belief that

God didn't come through for us. We get caught believing, *"There's something out there or someone better than what I have or who I have."*

Let's look at the verse above in the Book of Hebrews.
"Make every effort to live in peace with everyone and to be holy; without holiness no one will see the Lord. See to it that no one falls short of the grace of God and that no bitter root grows up to cause trouble and defile many." - Hebrews 12:14-15 (NIV)

Can Christians fall short of the glory of God? Yes, on the opposite of two spectrums.

☑ Legalism is the belief that puts principles in the place of God's grace.

☑ Licence is the belief that justifies immorality in the name of God's grace.

Let's take a closer look at them:

➤ *Lawlessness* - Evil or an evil living. The belief that I can live any way I want to without consequence. Paul reminds us that without holiness will never be in the presence of God (vs 14). It's easy to think this is talking about an unbeliever but this letter is written for the believer. He's warning them that we can miss ever being in the presence of God.

He challenges them, saying, *"Make every effort to be holy."*

The words, *"See the Lord"* doesn't mean to look at him. It means to see him face-to-face. You will never have an intimacy with the Lord. Yes, we receive holiness by grace through faith but we are also to walk holy as believers. It's not one or the other; it's both.

We can miss the presence of God because we are not walking in a holy lifestyle.

BALANCED Spiritual Life
(Rules + Relationship)

←→

Rules (without Relationship)

Relationship (without Rules)

> *Legalism* - puts principles in the place of God's grace.

Paul calls out the false teachers in Galatia who were preaching *"another Gospel."*

Their gospel went something like, "to be accepted one must believe upon the Son of God and be circumcised. In other words, those who were circumcised could, in some sense, depend on their religious work to justify them eternally before God."[16]

This infuriated Paul, so he calls them out in Galatians 2...

"So that is why I don't view God's grace as something minor or peripheral. For if keeping the law could release God's righteousness to us, the Anointed One would have died for nothing."

If salvation requires something to be added to it, then it is not real salvation. Legalism is trying to earn our Life in Christ. Paul goes on his letter to them...

"O you foolish and thoughtless and superficial Galatians, who has <u>bewitched you</u> [that you would act like this]," - (3:1 AMP)

The word bewitched is only used one time in scripture. The root of the word of *bewitched* is 'magic.' Paul is saying, *"Satan is trying to trick you to look someplace else so you won't see what he's doing right in front of your eyes."*

Bitterness is when the enemy get us focused on the wrong thing so we miss what God is doing right in front of us. We don't have

16 http://evangelicalfocus.com/magazine/3511/The_Pitfalls_of_Legalism_and_Licence

to buy into bitterness. We can be given the fruit of bitterness but we don't have to eat.

Jacob gave = He (Esau) ate (Genesis 25:34)

Eve gave = He (Adam) ate (Genesis 3:6)

THOUGHTS TODAY:

☑ When I become offended and don't deal with an offense the right way, it can grow into my soul and become a root of bitterness.

☑ If I allow unresolved conflict (the sprout) in my life, it will eventually become a deeply embedded thought (a root) in the way I think about them.

☑ Offenses will come, but the danger comes when I am not able to deal with them in a healthy way.

☑ Offense deceives me into believing my one meal of disobedience and bitterness is better than sitting at the table of forgiveness and abundance.

☑ Partial truth will always be the enemy's greatest weapon against me as a believer.

☑ If the enemy of my soul can get me to question God's character, then everything else will fall apart.

☑ My enemy wants my disappointments to grow into bitterness.

☑ Legalism is the belief that puts principles in the place of God's grace.

☑ License is the belief that justifies immorality in the name of God's grace.

Add Five Minutes to Your Study

 LEAN INTO LOVE

> "And do not give the devil an opportunity [to lead you into sin by holding a grudge, or nurturing anger, or harboring resentment, or cultivating bitterness]."
> - Ephesians 4:27 (AMP)

I love how the Amplified Bible gives us such practical application. Four distinct ways that we can be led into habits of sin:

1. Holding a grudge

2. Nurturing anger

3. Harboring resentment

4. Cultivating bitterness

I want you to consider one of the four areas you must struggle with in your everyday life. Is one of these in danger of growing a root in your foundation? Be really honest with yourself.

 TAKE THE LEAP

I want you to do this in private. Take out a piece of paper and a pen. Sit for a minute and ask the Holy Spirit to help you with this activation. Now, write down one or all of the names of the people in your life that you have struggled with offense toward. It could be an obvious breach. But it also doesn't have to be a major offense. It could be a disagreement or misunderstanding.

The point isn't the magnitude of what they did, but how it affected you.

It may even be something you already resolved, but it just seems to linger. After you've written each of these names, I want you to ask the Holy Spirit to help you forgive and release your offense. Weather it was intentional or unintentional isn't the main point. The point is the enemy can use any of these moments to fester bitterness. We are simply exposing him and his lies, and leaping into love.

Day Fifteen
REFLECTION DAY

RECORD: WHAT HAPPENED THIS WEEK FOR YOU?

_____

_____

_____

_____

_____

WHAT WAS YOUR PREVAILING EMOTION?

_____

_____

_____

_____

_____

_____

HAVE YOU EVER LEARNED ABOUT THIS BEFORE?

SKETCH: HOW WOULD YOU DRAW IT?

REFLECT: WHAT'S YOUR INTERPRETATION?

_____

_____

_____

_____

CONCLUSION: IN ONE SENTENCE, WRITE YOUR MOST
PROVOKING THOUGHT THAT WOULD MOVE YOU FORWARD:

_____

_____

_____

_____

THE PURPOSE
CHANGING CULTURE
Week Four

There's a story I want you to hear,

"A water bearer in China had two large pots, each hung on the ends of a pole which he carried across his neck. One of the pots had a crack in it, while the other pot was perfect and always delivered a full portion of water. At the end of the long walk from the stream to the house, the cracked pot arrived only half full.

For a full two years, this went on daily, with the bearer delivering only one and a half pots full of water to his house. Of course, the perfect pot was proud of its accomplishments, perfect for which it was made. But the poor cracked pot was ashamed of its own imperfection and miserable that it was able to accomplish only half of what it had been made to do.

After two years of what it perceived to be a bitter failure, it spoke to the water bearer one day by the stream. "I am ashamed of myself because this crack in my side causes water to leak out all the way back to your house."

The bearer said to the pot, "Did you notice that there were flowers only on your side of the path, but not on the other pot's side? That's because I have always known about your flaw, and I planted flower seeds on your side of the path, and every day while we walk back, you've watered them. For two years I have been able to pick these beautiful flowers to decorate the table. Without you being just the way you are, there would not be this beauty to grace the house."

What a parallel! I wonder how many of us go to God complaining about the parts of our lives that seem broken or incomplete? I wonder how much we've told God that our features, our talents, or our very existence seems to be less than the person next to us? I don't think I'm the only one who's ever felt like my life is less than significant. I've been caught gawking at the person next to me who seems to function in perfect proportion to their purpose.

So, what do we do? Sell everything. Move to a different island. Pray reincarnation is a real thing. Ha! Not so much. We can experience something profound. When everything can change and yet nothing changes. How? It's a simple word called perspective. Perspective is when we look at something from a different angle. I love this perspective was defined here.

"'Shift your perspective' – a phrase we often hear that refers to an observation or thinking practice. One definition: taking the way you think about a topic, setting that aside for a moment, and adopting another way to think about the very same topic. Reflecting on a topic in a new way is a great way to problem solve. Shifting or even combining perspectives makes our minds work on a problem differently. It illuminates new ways forward that we previously could not see." [17]

This week, we will work on shifting our perspective. I will show you the plan that could change your whole life if you're willing to attach your thoughts and beliefs. We will uncover how homegrown happiness is possible. We will reveal your hidden narratives, and show you how new core values can becoming. Lastly, we will see how you can propel forward towards becoming an agent of change in your everyday life.

So, let's get right to it! Grab your coffee, your bible, a good pen, and let's get started.

17 https://opencommunities.wordpress.com/2011/04/17/shift-your-perspective-on-diversity-terms/

HOMEGROWN HAPPINESS

(THE POWER OF OUR THOUGHTS)

> "Be happy in the moment, that's enough. Each moment is all we need, not more." - Mother Teresa

In my enthusiasm, I quickly grabbed the headband and placed it on my head. Beck was now laughing with excitement. But then the house continued in its full activity; backpacks being put away, lunch boxes emptied and shoes being thrown in the bin. I quickly got busy living in mom mode and didn't realize I'd left the headpiece on.

It wasn't until my husband walked in the door an hour later, when his eyes met mine and quickly trailed up to my head, did I realized I was still wearing Beck's project. We laughed as I slipped the headpiece off, but as I did Ben asked me what was on my forehead? I didn't know. As he walked closer to me, he reached his hand out to touch the mark.

Then he got that look in his eyes that told me something was very funny. I jumped up and ran into the bathroom to look in the mirror to see what he was grinning about.

When I could finally make out what the mark was, I realized it said MAHKCEB, Beckham spelled backward. Beckham had Sharpied his name on the inside of his headpiece.

Apparently, the ink wasn't dry and had permanently tattooed my head with Sharpie. It wouldn't come off! Trust me, I tried soap and water, scrubbing my forehead until it was red. But there was still evidence of his name.

Oh, the joys of motherhood!

It's been said that whatever the brain sits on, it will take its form. Just like Beckham's name sitting on my forehead, whatever rests on our minds, shapes our lives. The longer it sits there, the harder it is to get off.

Being *fully present to our purpose on the planet* will always come down to acknowledging our happiness isn't an outside job, but rather a deep inward work. I call it *homegrown happiness!* **We can create homegrown happiness.**

I grow Homegrown HAppiness

If we can change the way we think about life, we can change the way we feel about life, and ultimately our actions will follow the truth about what we believe about life.

Your thoughts are the most powerful weapon for life change. We can't have a healthy life and still have an unhealthy thought life. Likewise, we can't have a healthy life without seeing the results of health in our everyday living. Today I want us to look at how we can grow happiness in our everyday life. It's possible to be happier than you've ever been.

What do you think about this phrase?

"God wants to help you live the abundant life without anyone else participating."

This may be hard to imagine, since we are so often waiting for something or someone to show up so we can fully be present. Trust me, I'm as guilty as the next person! I found myself waiting on someone or something for years of my life believing that "when" they change, then "we" will change. What I didn't realize was that the moment I started waiting for them to show up, I was giving away my power: the power to partner with the Holy Spirit.

Jesus said in John 10:10, *"I've come to give you life and life abundantly."*

We don't get abundant life when our spouse gets it together, or when a leader acknowledges us. Life doesn't start when one of our teenage children begins serving God. No, Jesus said we can have abundant life today, if we really want it.

Abundant life begins first in the mind.

I want us to visit Romans chapter 12.
"And do not be conformed to this world [any longer with its superficial values and customs], but be transformed and progressively changed [as you mature spiritually] by the renewing of your mind [focusing on godly values and ethical attitudes], so that you may prove [for yourselves] what the will of God is, that which is good and acceptable and perfect [in His plan and purpose for you]." - Romans 12:2 (AMP)

There are a few things we need to focus on in this passage.

1. Transformation is a <u>progressive</u> process.

    It doesn't happen overnight. You will need to keep moving forward. Transformation is a forward movement.

2. Transformation <u>reveals</u> spiritual maturity.

If there's no proof then it's ok to question if it's actually real. If you can't see the growth, then are you really growing anything?

3. Transformation happens when we focus our attention on godly _values_ and _ethics_.

   Your _Values_ - are principles of behavior that are important to you.

   Your _Ethics_ - govern those values by your behavior.

   Transformation focuses your attention on what's important to you by aligning your behavior with what you believe.

If I want to lose weight, it will require transformation. First, I have to find my "_why_." Why is this important to me? Second, I have to adjust my life by changing my behavior. What do I need to do each and every day to keep moving forward?

Romans 12 tells us that it is our responsibility to transform our mind. For some of us, that may not seem difficult. But for others (insert my hand raised), my mind seems to be the biggest battlefield in my life.

Let's examine this process further.

The power comes when we acknowledge that our thoughts have been leading us into negative and destructive patterns. It's one of the biggest hindrances to growing our life in God on purpose.

WE Think → WE FEEL → WE DO → ALL THE TIME → Our Life

How do we begin to build healthy self-accepting thoughts?

"On average, about a third of a person's strengths are innate, built into his or her genetically based temperament, talents, mood, and personality. The other two-thirds are developed over time. You get them by growing them."16

I love that this phrase says, "growing them," because that's exactly what we have to do. That's why the Bible challenges us to take every thought captive.

"We demolish arguments and every pretension that sets itself up against the knowledge of God, and we take captive every thought to make it obedient to Christ." - 2 Corinthians 10:5 (NIV)

Do you remember on Day 12 when we talked about transformation? I mentioned how the tension between *self-awareness* and *spiritual awakening* can often lead me to feel anxious. The same process is needed in order to train our minds.

At first, taking every thought captive can feel *exhausting* . . . *daunting*.

Imagine the effort it would take to challenge every negative thought that came into your head. It can seem overwhelming! It requires significant focus, but eventually it will become a habit and even a way of life.

Here's how transformation works in our thought-life.

I wrote about this in my book, *The Good Stuff: A Guidebook to Finishing Strong*.

"He gives us hope in all of this! He uses the word 'transformed' which gives us an understanding of how this happens. (Romans 12)

16 https://www.psychologytoday.com/us/blog/your-wise-brain/201410/grow-inner-strengths

This is another Greek word metamorphoo. You may recognize it — it is from the same word that we get the word 'metamorphosis'. It describes a comprehensive change, one so extensive it's like a caterpillar changing into a butterfly! Doesn't this give you hope? The fact is, our minds are not changed immediately and our thoughts do not change overnight. However, if we apply God's Word to our lives, with faith in our hearts, it will happen over time. Our thoughts will begin to line up with His thoughts and our mind becomes renewed! It's only a matter of time. So much of what God does in us is not an immediate work, but a work that happens over time; requiring trust, obedience, reliance, and perseverance. It's a relational work, not just a restorative effort. He wants to partner with us and teach us about Himself in the process."

HERE'S A SIMPLE ACTIVITY TO HELP YOU RENEW YOUR MIND.

- Purchase spiral bound, 3 x 5 inch, ruled, white Index Cards. You can find them in a grocery store for a little under $2.

- On the front of each card, write down the negative thoughts that plague your everyday life. Don't filter them. Be as honest as you can.

When I was renewing my thoughts and using this card system.

I wrote down thoughts like this:

- *"I'm not a good mom."*

- *"I'm not a great wife."*

- *"I can't do anything right."*

- "I'm running out of time."

Even though I knew in my head those were wrong thoughts, I had to be honest that they were still infecting my thought life.

- On the other side of the card, I wrote the truth about what God says.

- It could be a scripture, a truth that's biblical, or simply a promise God gave me. The point is to replace a negative thought with a God thought. It's not enough to just try and not do something; we need an alternative.

Over time, I memorized these truths and each time the enemy tries and get me to believe a lie, I repeat the truth over my life. Eventually these true thoughts became more real than the lies I've believed.

The more healthy and whole we become, the happier we are. It's not automatic, but it is authentic and homegrown.

THOUGHTS FOR TODAY:

- ☑ Whatever the mind rests on, it will take its form.

- ☑ I can create homegrown happiness.

- ☑ My thoughts are the most powerful weapon for life change.

- ☑ God wants to help me live the abundant life without anyone else participating.

- ☑ Transformation doesn't happen overnight, so I must keep moving forward. Transformation is a forward movement.

- ☑ If I can't see the growth, then am I really growing anything?

- ☑ Transformation focuses my attention on what's important to me by aligning my behavior with what I believe.

- ☑ The more healthy and whole I become, the happier I am.

Add Five Minutes to Your Study:

 LEAN INTO LOVE

> "So this is why we abandon everything morally impure and all forms of wicked conduct. Instead, with a sensitive spirit we absorb God's Word, which has been implanted within our nature, for the Word of Life has power to continually deliver us." - James 1:21 (TPT)

Another version of the Bible says, *"Therefore lay aside..."*[19] Lay aside means to lay something down, push it far away and move it beyond reach. It comes from the Greek word *apotithimi*. When James uses this same word for morally impure and wicked conduct, he's addressing these unhealthy attitudes as if they were dirty clothes. It's clear he's telling us to, *"GET THEM OFF!"*

When it comes to laying aside these unwholesome attitudes of the mind, it's ALL about removing the filthy garments we've become accustomed to. Not just taking them off when we want to, and then putting them back on later, but removing them once and for all. Throwing them out of reach!

 TAKE THE LEAP

One key to developing a healthy mind is having a renewed and edified spirit. If you have a supernatural prayer language, practice praying in the Spirit under your breath whenever you aren't speaking to someone else. If you don't pray in tongues, that's okay, just pray from your spirit man and worship the Lord under your breath. When our minds are engaged in prayer we're less likely to wander mentally and are more able to fill our minds with spiritual thoughts.

SELF-NARRATIVES
(THE POWER OF OUR WORDS)

> "Everything can be taken from a man but one thing: the last of the human freedoms—to choose one's attitude in any given set of circumstances, to choose one's own way."
> - Viktor E. Frank

A few months ago I wrote this on my Instagram. I was surprised by the response.

Here's what I wrote:

"I'm just going to get it out there: TODAY IS MY BIRTHDAY."

NARRATIVE #1

"I hate my body. I can't lose weight. I can't lose the stretch marks. I'll never be able to go back to what I was. It's too late. I should have been more disciplined. Maybe then I wouldn't feel so humiliated by the way I look."

NARRATIVE #2

"I'm proud of my body. It's been good to me. It gave me four little humans; four brains, four faces, four boys. I'm grateful for the marks on my body. They prove I've lived. The extra weight represents the croissants I ate with the love of my life in Paris. The cookie I ate because Beckham made it for me. The donuts we splurged on because we are a family, and family celebrates life together. I can change. I can focus on getting stronger; living longer by making better

choices. I'm not going to be what I was, but I'm going to be the best/ healthiest version of myself."

NARRATIVE #1

"I hate getting old. I feel more tired at night. I don't know what's cool anymore. The guy at the grocery store calls me "Ma'am." I have a hard time recognizing myself in pictures. I look more tired than I feel. My skin is sagging. My hair is turning grey. I'm not a young mom. I should have started earlier. The best is behind me."

NARRATIVE #2

"I'm aging with grace. Grace to be older. Grace to be the oldest in the room. Grace to let my body age without anger. I don't have to look young to be beautiful. I'm the right mom for my kids. My life is like a well-worn shoe. I like it; it's comfortable. It's me. Bleach that grey. Drink water. Dance more. Rock a one piece. It's normal to age. You're normal."

NARRATIVE #1

"I'm running out of time. I wish I would have felt this comfortable in my 20's. Why is it when you finally have the money and wisdom, you are halfway done with life? This is as good as it's going to get. I've peaked. I wish I could pause life right here. The loss is coming."

NARRATIVE #2

"I'm right on time. I'm comfortable with my life because I've worked hard to build the one I want. Older people are happier in life. They look at you in the eyes. They have time. I have time. What I'm supposed to do, I will do. "

 WHAT'S YOUR NARRATIVE TODAY?

These words resonated with many of you. And I get it... sometimes perspective gives us the courage to move forward. I wonder how many times in our lives we got caught believing the wrong narrative?

A few weeks ago a friend came to me. She confessed, *"I'm kind of embarrassed about this but during a meeting today, I started to feel really insecure. It's stupid, but as we were planning our next big event, the person in charge started to vision cast. They quickly went around the table placing specific individuals in distinct roles. I noticed she never mentioned me."*

If we change the Narrative, we change our lives.

I knew this wasn't like her so I began to ask her a few questions, trying to get a better picture of what was happening. She quickly answered my questions, but in a way that communicated back, *"It's okay, I'm already over it."*

But again, it was unlike her to divulge such a vulnerable moment. I wanted to see if there was more. I asked if I could ask another question. She agreed. *"Do you usually feel insecure with this group of people?"* To which she answered, *"Actually, no, not at all. I usually feel really comfortable with them and they seem to champion most of my ideas."*

This got me thinking.

Maybe there was more to this than just them dismissing her.

"Do you think they are really clear on what you bring to the table? If they were to say this is her expertise, would they quickly have an answer?" Her eyes now looking off in the distance, she said, *"I'm not really sure they do. I don't think I've ever really told them what I want to offer them or even feel competent in doing."*

I was now getting a clearer picture. She was an extremely competent woman. Full of expertise, but a little on the passive side. Easily accommodating.

Reader: Please don't let my description bother you. Passive is wonderful, but you'll see why this characteristic wasn't helping her at this very moment.

I challenged her with this thought,

"I don't think it was insecurity you were experiencing. I believe it was a moment of self awareness. You were suddenly aware they did not truly see the whole version of you. You wanted them to see your authentic self." Your inner being was trying to make an appearance.

Her Bio: She was born a middle child, with a very strong older sibling who tended to dominate. She was the peacemaker of the family. The 'easy child.' Often going along with anything anyone wanted to do and it had served her up until this point.

But after a lot of spiritual growth, self-awareness, and learning to be present to her purpose, her true self was emerging in the midst of her everyday life.

It would've been easy to brush off this moment as insecurity, quickly feeling ashamed but choosing to move on. Or, she could choose to hear the message inside of her that said, *"There is more to me then what I am presenting to the world."*

As this realization emerged, her eyes filled up with tears. She'd never processed these emotions with self-awareness rather than insecurity. I posed the question, *"What if the next time you felt this way, instead of feeling ashamed or overlooked, and labeling it as insecurity, what if you were more curious? Could you validate your emotions about feeling overlooked or misunderstood, and ask yourself better questions? Questions like: Why am I feeling this emotion or what could also be true at this moment? Could you stand up for the person you want to be by communicating your personal preference?"*

We talked a little longer and, eventually, she concluded, *"I think the next time I'm with this particular leader I'm going to spend a few minutes communicating what I really want to do. What I want to bring to the table."* She was beginning to understand her responsibility to communicate. Her duty to own how she was going to show up in the world around her. Her authentic self. She couldn't control the outcome, but she could thoroughly control her response to life.

I left our lunch feeling a sense of heightened emotion. I felt empathy for her, knowing without our conversation, she would have filed away this moment as negative, even adding shame to her story. I felt proud of her for being willing to talk to me about it, change the narrative, and leave empowered.

But I also felt emotion directed toward myself. I, too, had been quick to file away past emotions as moral or immoral, good or bad, selfish or unselfish. Rather than allowing myself to be curious about the person God created long before the Earth ever spun into motion. How many times had I just believed the narrative, rather than challenging the nature of it?

I want to live belonging to God. I want to embrace the person God created me to be. I don't want to belong to someone else's idea of what I should or shouldn't be.

So how do we show up in the world around us as our authentic self?

How do I stay true to who God has created me to be?

We change the narrative.

We challenge the narratives we've received from parents or influencers, religious leaders or society. We do the work of looking deep inside of our own insecurities or lack of authenticity and we begin to see there is another narrative that's truer than the one we've always heard.

The truth: We will always have two narratives that follow our lives.

The first narrative will always be filled with facts.

The fact: Half of my life is over + I'm never going to be as cute as I was + I've never made the money I thought I was worthy of + I never married the right person + I never had a loving Dad.

But, simultaneously, there is a second narrative that follows our lives as believers. It's the narrative of truth. Truth tells us there is a possibility in the middle of the impossible.

The truth: It's never too late + God will make a way + I'm just getting started + my best is yet to come + I have the most loving Creator.

We don't ignore the facts. That's delusional. We simply don't let them have the final word. We have a God narrative that's set before us every day. The choice is ours to what narrative we will believe.

I quickly think about the scripture that says,

"I call heaven and earth as witnesses against you today, that I have set before you life and death, the blessing and the curse; therefore, you shall choose life in order that you may live, you and your descendants, Each day we have a narrative. A narrative of life or narrative of death." - Deuteronomy 30:19 (AMP)

Our time together is coming to an end in a couple of days so I want to be straight with you. No one is responsible for the narrative you believe, other than yourself. Stop blaming your parents, your leaders, your boss, your spouse or anyone other than yourself. You are so POWERFUL! You have the power to choose what God says about you whether the facts line up or not.

This quote stuck with me years after I'd first read it. It was said by a man who lived through the Holocaust.

"Everything can be taken from a man but one thing: the last of the human freedoms—to choose one's attitude in any given set of circumstances, to choose one's own way." - Viktor E. Frankl

WOW! It's hard to even process but even in the face of a living hell, they still could choose their internal narrative.

Even Paul said,

"Yet in all these things we are more than conquerors and gain an overwhelming victory through Him who loved us [so much that He died for us]. 38 For I am convinced [and continue to be convinced—beyond any doubt] that neither death, nor life, nor angels, nor principalities, nor things present and threatening, nor things to come, nor powers, 39 nor height, nor depth, nor any other created thing, will be able to separate us from the [unlimited] love of God, which is in Christ Jesus our Lord." - Romans 8:37-39 (AMP)

Paul was a man who chose his truth narrative.

Was he a Christian killer himself? *Yes.*

Did he deserve to have a good life? *Nope, not at all.*

But Paul chose God's narrative over his life, rather than what the facts were about him.

Another passage comes to mind,

"There will be a highway called the Holy Road. No one rude or rebellious is permitted on this road. It's for God's people exclusively—impossible to get lost on this road. Not even fools can get lost on it. No lions on this road, no dangerous wild animals—Nothing and no one dangerous or threatening. Only the redeemed will walk on it. The people God has ransomed will come back on this road. They'll sing as they make their way home to Zion, unfading halos of joy encircling their heads, welcomed home with gifts of joy and gladness as all sorrows and sighs scurry into the night." - Isaiah 35:8-10 (MSG)

We know that most people won't choose this road.

Even Jesus said, **"Enter through the narrow gate. For wide is the gate and broad and easy to travel is the path that leads the way to destruction and eternal loss, and there are many who enter through it." - Matthew 7:13 (AMP)**

The narrative of the world is easy to believe. After all, it's the enemy's way of keeping us small, irrelevant and unproductive. And it's not hard to believe this narrative because the facts line up. The truth is public. Our time is running out.

But each day we have a choice to walk on the narrow road. The road that few people take, but will lead us to life. We will walk through valleys, climb mountains, scale cliffs, trudge through deserts, but as long as our destination is set, our truth narrative is in Heaven's facts.

THOUGHTS FOR TODAY:

☑ If I change my narrative, I change my life.

☑ I can't control the outcome, but I can thoroughly control my response to life.

☑ How many times have I believed the narrative, rather than challenging the nature of it?

☑ I need to do the work of looking deep inside my own insecurities or lack of authenticity. Only then can I begin to see there is another narrative that's truer than the one I've always heard.

☑ Truth tells me there is a possibility in the middle of the impossible.

☑ I don't ignore the facts. I simply don't let them have the final word.

☑ I have the power to choose what God says about me whether the facts line up or not.

☑ My truth narrative is Heaven's facts.

Add Five Minutes to Your Study

 LEAN INTO LOVE

> "Come to God through the narrow gate, because the wide gate and broad path is the way that leads to destruction— nearly everyone chooses that crowded road!"
> Matthew 7:13 (TPT)

"...nearly everyone chooses that crowded road!" That's a chilling thought. Most of the messaging you get on a daily basis is directed at those on the crowded road. But you will have to choose to walk through the narrow gate. Facts are easy to follow but truth is a gate that's hard to follow but leads to unending promises.

 TAKE THE LEAP

Take a moment today to write out the narrative you have been believing about your life. Be honest. Get it all out. Under the "facts" narrative, write out your "truth narrative." Ask God to help you believe what He says about you today.

My Narrative...

Day Eighteen
THE NON-NEGOTIABLE ME
(HARDWIRED TO BE ME)

The fires had reached the edge of the city. It wasn't uncommon for us to have fires, specifically in Northern California. Another fire simply meant it was Fire Season. It was progressively getting worse. but no one stopped to think the fire might actually enter our city.

We'd been staying at a friend's house. They were kind enough to open up their home after our air conditioning gave out right in the middle of summer. Summers in Redding get so hot you could fry an egg on the pavement. We were on a 10-day run with temperatures reaching over 100°. So we'd packed the kids up, took our friends up on their offer, and moved into their air-conditioned home on the west side of town.

The fires were roaring up by Whiskeytown Lake, about 10 miles from where we were staying. Evacuations had reached the outer limits of the city now, but those in town seemed to still navigate their everyday lives. That evening, we picked up dinner and headed back to the house to watch a movie. The air quality was extremely dangerous so we were relegated to living indoors.

As we were sitting in our friend's living room watching a movie together, the lights flickered a couple of times. And then at one moment, the entire electricity went out and came back on. You could hear all of the energy starting up again. Ben and I looked at each other. This wasn't a good sign.

 I said, *"I think we should get out of here,"* and Ben quickly agreed. We jumped up to grab our things, beginning to clean up. As I walked around the corner into their kitchen, I immediately froze. Her wall to wall windows, overlooking the green hills, were filled with flames. I immediately asked Ben to come and see what I was witnessing. As he rounded the corner he blurted, *"You get the kids, and I'll get our stuff."*

I quickly loaded our kids in the car. I was trying to keep calm, but I'm not sure I was succeeding. Calling my friend, the owner of the house, who was currently spending the summer in San Diego with her family, I wanted to know if I could grab anything for her in case they were going to lose their home.

Actually, we'd been texting all day but hadn't yet connected to get her *"must-have"* list. At this point, I was desperately trying to reach her.

On our final trip into the house, she answered. At the sound of her voice, *"Havilah!"* I immediately burst into tears. Through my tears, I told her we were leaving her home and asked if there was anything important we needed to grab. I was borderline hysterical at this point. She calmly said, *"Just grab anything you think, but there is something you can get for me."* She asked me to go into the guest room and find a basket on the top shelf of the closet. I listened intently.

Walking into the guest bedroom and straight to the closet, I reached for the basket. The basket was full of baby clothes. I thought, *"Oh! She must want these baby clothes."* She continued.

"Dump all those clothes out and at the bottom of the basket, you'll find a blue envelope." I did exactly that, and was now standing in the closet holding a blue envelope. She quickly asked me to open it and see if there was money in it. I unzipped the envelope, and could now see hundreds of dollars in a pile.

I quickly blurted out without thinking, *"Michelle, are you guys drug dealers?"* to which we both laughed. Her response, *"No, I just forgot to make a deposit for the business."* She had me grab a few more things; pictures, a computer hard drive, papers.

Within minutes we were pulling away from the house with all of her belongings in a small cardboard box. Driving out of the neighborhood, you could feel the panic in the area. We were now in bumper to bumper traffic as we left the community. Fire trucks were coming on the opposite side of the road, driving into the fire.

We went back to our house to promptly grab our belongings. The fire was so erratic at this point, moving straight for our city, jumping rivers like hopscotch. It was so unpredictable we didn't even know if our house was in jeopardy. So we drove back to our home and ran inside to grab our stuff; family albums, pictures, passports, documents, my grandmother's prom dress, treasured Christmas ornaments; as much as we could fit in the car.

The last time we went into our house the power was now cut off. We jumped into our cars, now filled with four kids, a dog and all of our belongings. Honestly, it was happening so fast, it was hard to even process the moment. As we drove away, I thought, *"This could be the last time we ever see our home."*

We drove through the night to El Dorado Hills, pulling into Mom and Dad's driveway at 3 o'clock in the morning, with our belongings and Michelle's in our two cars, parked out front.

Climbing into bed, a wave of relief and emotion hit me all at once. Of course, I started to remember all the things I should've grabbed, even the things I could've grabbed if I'd thought of them. But it was too late, what we had was what we had.

That week was devastating for our community. Many of our friends and families lost their homes. It was crushing for our small city. But both Michelle's home and our home were spared, leaving us deeply grateful for the men and women who fought the fire so well.

As I think about this moment in time, I'm struck with the reality that in the middle of life, in the middle of chaos and trauma, things get really clear. What's important to you are really the only things you take with you. My thoughts while walking through my house was simple, *"That's replaceable... we can buy that again... it's all just stuff."* But there are other things that, if lost, would be entirely devastating. Losing a child, a spouse, a sibling, a parent or a friend, would change my whole life, affecting my ability to live, damaging my ability to remember who I am, or even where I've been. Utter loss.

Much like this, there are things in our lives we must take with us everywhere we go. It doesn't matter how much struggle, trauma, rebuilding or repurposing we would have to do. We need specific items in order to stay grounded.

Healthy.

Whole.

If lost, we would have to create a whole new normal.

We'd lose a piece of ourselves.

In our lives, we call them core values. They are the things we must have with us. They must be protected. No matter what environment, relationship, city, or age we find ourselves in, they are with us. Our core values keep us grounded.

Honest. Authentic. Healthy. Alive.

Today, I want us to look at some essential core values we must have in our lives in order to live fully present to our purpose on the planet. Without any one of these, we will be missing a vital piece. We may even find ourselves devastated, disillusioned or destitute without them.

ESSENTIAL CORE VALUES TO OUR PURPOSE

 ### I LIVE FOR A HIGHER PURPOSE

It's impossible to live with a purpose if you don't see life from an elevated position. It's like trying to figure out where you are without having a map. Have you ever been lost in a city? You may be able to navigate parts of it, but you'll never be quite sure where you are. It's not until you go to the top floor of a high rise and look down;only then do you understand where you've been, where you are standing and where you want to go.

I think about the Psalmist who said,

"He stooped down to lift me out of danger from the desolate pit I was in, out of the muddy mess I had fallen into. Now he's lifted me up into a firm, secure place and steadied me while I walk along his ascending path." - Psalm 40:2 (TPT)

Our purpose comes from a higher place. You are called to live for a greater mission.

PURPOSE DOESN'T COME FROM:

- ☑ Living for the weekends

- ☑ Funding your kid's college fund

- ☑ Proficient in a personal interest

- ☑ Living to make someone else happy

- ☑ Creating the perfect life

- ☑ Winning every argument

- ☑ Standing on a stage

Your purpose connects to a higher eternal plan. God's purpose for your life is that you would demonstrate who He is to the Earth around you; to be known, to, and to make Him known. These relationships are our highest purpose!

Think about the words of Peter,

**"But you are the ones chosen by God, chosen for the high calling of priestly work, chosen to be a holy people, God's instruments to do his work and speak out for him, to tell others of the night-and-day difference he made for you— from nothing to something, from rejected to accepted."
- 1 Peter 2:9-10 (MSG)**

Only when we understand that we are living for a higher purpose, do we stay grounded in the small and insignificant parts of our lives, as well as the seemingly grand moments too. We understand each moment is significant to God's purpose for our mission. It's when we finally realize our purpose will never be about *"what we do,"* but in *"who we are"* while doing it.

Our life is like a beautiful picture. For different parts to stand out and make a difference, we have to have the dull and colorless parts to life simultaneously. It's what makes life rich!

 **I AM VALUABLE**

Celebrating my existence is the deep work of self-acceptance. True acceptance is rejecting what my enemy wants me to believe — the lie that God cheated me when He made me this way. Nope, I'm not buying it! I'm embracing the person God created me to be without disappointment, fear or anger.

Spirit-led acceptance is grounded in the hope that our Creator God isn't finished making and molding me. I am valuable. Actually, invaluable to Him. God designed my features to line up with His plan for my life. Every part of me was created on purpose, to look a specific way, and for a critical mission.

My unchangeable features will always tell the story of my Creator. **"I praise you because I am fearfully and wonderfully made; your works are wonderful, I know that full well." - Psalm 139:14 (NIVUK)**
My enemy is hoping I believe there is only one defined Universal Beauty, but He is a liar.

I am beautiful.

Created perfectly.

I'm learning to agree with God about myself. I'm redefining my flaws as marks of ownership reminding me of Whom I belong to. There is no 'ideal outward beauty,' only an 'ideal inward beauty' seen by God alone. My purpose will never be to be beautiful. My mission is to emulate the image of Christ on the planet. That, to Him, is the most beautiful thing I could ever do.

♡ I AM FULL OF POTENTIAL

Reaching my potential is becoming the best version of the person God created me to be; nothing more, and nothing less. Only God can show me my missing pieces, revealing my true worth and value. Healthy things will always grow!

Only when I am plugged into my source, can I live my authentic self. I have an unlimited source of comfort, connection, and confidence which comes from the inside of me, through the relationship with the Holy Spirit. Jesus must be the center of my whole life.

♡ I AM IN PROCESS

When my personality becomes the source of my identity, I lose contact with my spirit and my deep connection with God. When I connect with the person God created me to be, the  work of transformation begins. When I am busy performing for the picture inside my head, I know deep down that I am not entirely being authentic. The more I perform for others, the more I am not true to myself, and merely belong to their picture of me. Transformation will always be a journey, never a destination.

In order for me to live a spiritually awakened life, and sustain a healthy, spiritual path, I will need to work out my salvation. (Philippians 2:12) When I begin to see all the promises God has given me and the access I have to them, I begin to let go of my soulish wisdom.

God mercifully works to redeem every painful circumstance in my life. I am convinced that every detail of my life, even my flaws, can be woven together to fit in God's perfect plan. I can only change when my willingness to accept God-allowed pain exceeds my fears. Self-awareness will always be the gateway to breakthrough.

THOUGHTS FOR TODAY:

- ☑ It's essential that I have core values in order to live fully present to my purpose on the planet.

- ☑ My core values keep me grounded.

- ☑ It's impossible to live with a purpose if I don't see life from an elevated position.

- ☑ God's purpose for my life is that I would demonstrate who He is to the Earth around me.

- ☑ It's when I finally realize my purpose will never be about "what I do," but in "Who I am" while doing it.

- ☑ Celebrating my existence is the deep work of self-acceptance.

- ☑ Every part of me was created on purpose, to look a specific way and for a critical mission.

- ☑ My mission is to emulate the image of Christ on the planet.

- ☑ Jesus must be the center of my whole life.

Add Five Minutes to Your Study

LEAN INTO LOVE

> "I pray with great faith for you, because I'm fully convinced that the One who began this glorious work in you will faithfully continue the process of maturing you and will put his finishing touches to it until the unveiling of our Lord Jesus Christ!" - Philippians 1:6 (TPT)

One of my core values is - I Am in Process. This one took me a long time to understand. I wanted to finish. Complete. I didn't realize that it's BOTH/AND. The work of the cross is complete. I've got everything I need to begin my journey, but I still need to follow the trail. I finished, and I'm just starting too.

The process could feel daunting until we understand we didn't start this work, nor will we be responsible for finishing it. "The One who began this glorious work in you will faithfully continue the process..." We can find comfort that we didn't start this transformation in our lives and we don't have to complete it. Our creator is the author and the finisher.

TAKE THE LEAP

Today, I want you to find a way to get these core values in front of you. Maybe you're an artist and can draw them. Some of you can print them up and tape them to your mirror. While others can journal about them or even make a digital screen saver. The point is that you meditate on these core truths and make them a part of your life.

P.S. You might be inspired to add a few I didn't mention. On the next page, write the ones I've given you, but feel free to add your own in there.

Core Values

> "I am only one, but still I am one. I cannot do everything, but still, I can do something; and because I cannot do everything, I will not refuse to do something that I can do."
> - Helen Keller

I know many of you aren't aware of my story. I wrote about it in this excerpt from my book, **Stronger Than The Struggle: Uncomplicating Your Spiritual Battle.**

"I grew up with learning disabilities. I was not good at reading or writing, and I was always terribly embarrassed about it. In fact, I spent most of my time trying to hide my struggle. I became super social to cover up my inability to perform academically and my subsequent humiliation. Heightening my sense of inferiority, I had an identical twin who was excellent in all the areas where I was subpar.

I would go to school and feel inadequate, then I would go to church and feel the exact same way. I had been raised in the church, but I always felt pretty lost there. Actually, I felt a little lost in general. I did not have a natural, unique leadership gifting. I wasn't the person who was asked to do a lot in my community. I was the girl who flew under the radar, always overlooked and always dreaming, hoping I would one day be exceptional at something. I often thought that I just needed one big win—a triumph to confirm my value. Something that would make the struggle within me worth it. Maybe I thought success would make life easier and give me the inner confidence I so lacked.

Little did I know that my internal battle—which I so hoped to throw off—would shape and influence my purpose and direction in life."

Making assumptions is easy. I'm as guilty as the next person. But when we make assumptions about others (or I like to say, 'fill in facts'), it robs us at our core. Blocking our ability to learn and stay curious about someone else's story.

I shared this portion from my book to help you understand that what I'm about to tell you did not come easy for me.

I want you to hear me when I say I never came from a position of being ahead of others but rather starting with a feeling of being so behind I couldn't imagine catching up, let alone leading in the topic. But since it's our last day, I'm going to get straight to the point.

HERE ARE SOME FACTS ABOUT YOU:

☑ You Are an Agent of Change

☑ You Are a World Changer

☑ You Are a Leader

☑ You Are A Vital Voice

You may never have been called these names before, but that doesn't make it any less accurate. When God formed you in the womb, He wanted you to be a part of His ridiculously fantastic plan. You are an essential soul to His mission. Your presence matters!

My favorite quote says,

"Just you being born is evidence you possess something this generation needs." - Anonymous

You were born to be a leader. Your presence is essential to the kingdom of God. For you to see yourself as a leader, you may have to redefine what a leader encompasses.

I've got to give it to the Urban Dictionary for a winning definition. It says,

"A leader is someone who has the ability to inspire others to achieve tasks and goals that they might not otherwise be capable of reaching."

In a world which often gives leadership to the outgoing personality or forceful voice, none of these qualities is a prerequisite for leadership. Leadership comes from those willing to become an example. Those willing to change the culture around them by merely **starting with themselves.**

How do we encourage others to live present to their purpose on the planet? We acknowledge, *"It starts with me."* I have a sign hanging up in my house that says, ***"You have to be brave with your life so that others can be brave with theirs."*** Courage is transferred when we emulate courage.

When I was 17 years old, I attended my youth group at church. I was beginning my wholehearted walk with Christ. After some time, I'd set up a meeting with my youth pastor to express some of my thoughts about our community. Mostly, I wanted to share that me and a few of my friends were frustrated that our worship pastor (who was old back then...a whole 35 years) was leading worship for our youth group, and we wanted someone more our age.

I wasn't completely innocent. A few friends and I had started a small band. As I expressed intensely that we needed to have people our age leading worship, my youth pastor listened intently. I assumed he would challenge my frustration, defending his choice to have worship led by this particular person. Instead, he looked across the desk at me and said, *"Okay, great, why don't you and your band lead worship next week?"* I'm not sure I hid the shock in my face as I tried to absorb what he just said. I was equally terrified, but up for the challenge.

When I got home that day, I quickly called the band, explaining that we would be making a public appearance that next week at youth group. We crammed in sessions that week to practice our skills, and arrived a whole two hours early that night for sound check.

Our friends and classmates filled the small room as we led our first worship set. And it was...HORRIBLE! Let's just say: we needed a whole lot more practice. But, simultaneously, something extraordinary happened.

As we were leading, I felt compelled to interrupt the moment to explain how God felt about them. Tears streamed down my face, as I encouraged them about God's plan for their lives. I turned to my bandmates to see they were emotional as well. God was up to something.

It wasn't pretty.

Far from perfect.

But it was a moment in time where God's presence was acknowledged and souls were awakened.

I spent two years leading worship for my youth group and eventually spending eight years of my life as a worship pastor of our church. My simple choice led to helping thousands of people experience the presence of God. But it all goes back to that moment in the youth pastor's room when he called my bluff. I had a choice to make. Was I willing to show up, even if it wasn't perfect? Would I look at life head-on? Would I be present for this moment of purpose on the planet? It's easy to look back now and think, *"Well, of course, I would. Look at what I've been able to accomplish with God all these years."* But remember. I had no knowledge of the future. I was just will to lead a few songs for a group of 30 peers.

Living as an Agent of Change isn't about having everything perfectly outlined so we can step into our cushy calling. It's always about doing the next thing in front of us as best we can. I like to say, *"Favor comes when you are the best you are wherever you are."*

Yesterday we talked about life's essentials; the things we need to take with us no matter where we go. Let's look at what it takes to be a world changer.

3 ESSENTIAL CORE VALUES TO CHANGE AGENTS

1. My Life Counts.

2. My Presence Matters.

3. I Believe in the Power of One.

The last one should be pretty easy for us to believe since it's the core of our gospel.

The Power of One, Jesus Christ, changed everything.

"In God's economy, one man redeemed the world by stretching out his arms and giving of himself a perfect sacrifice for us all. This was one man." - Abagail Nelson

How do we change the culture? We start right where we are:

- ☑ We celebrate the girl who is trying on clothes in the dressing room.

- ☑ We smile at the prettiest girl at the table.

- ☑ We compliment the little girl who waltzes by us in the park.

- ☑ We stop encouraging universal beauty, and we start celebrating unique expressions of beauty.

- ☑ We value the character of God demonstrated in someone's life rather than just beautiful attributes and full features.

I love the quote, *"Too often we underestimate the power of a touch, a smile, a kind word, a listening ear, an honest compliment, or the smallest act of caring, all of which have the potential to turn a life around."*

So today, be a world changer! Say *"Yes"* to life's challenges. Lean into love. Stay present.

THOUGHTS FOR TODAY:

- ☑ Making assumptions blocks my ability to learn and stay curious about someone else's story.

- ☑ I am an Agent of Change.

- ☑ I am a World Changer.

- ☑ I am a Leader.

☑ I am a Vital Voice.

☑ I'm an essential soul to God's mission.

☑ Leadership comes from those willing to become an example.

☑ Courage is transferred when I emulate courage.

☑ Living as an Agent of Change is always about doing the next thing in front of me, as best I can.

☑ My Life Counts.

☑ My Presence Matters.

☑ I Believe in the Power of One.

Add Five Minutes to Your Study

 LEAN INTO LOVE

> "As a prisoner of the Lord, I plead with you to walk holy, in a way that is suitable to your high rank, given to you in your divine calling." - Ephesians 4:1 (TPT)

Paul is challenging Timothy in this passage to live worthy of his calling. But this challenge is for us too. We're to live worthy of the calling we've received. Worthy of the potential we possess. I love how the message paraphrases this passage.

"...I want you to get out there and walk—better yet, run!—on the road God called you to travel. I don't want any of you sitting around on your hands. I don't want anyone strolling off, down some path that goes nowhere. And mark that you do this with humility and discipline—not in fits and starts, but steadily, pouring yourselves out for each other in acts of love, alert at noticing differences and quick at mending fences." - Ephesians 4:1-3 (MSG)

 TAKE THE LEAP

Today I want you to get this message in front of you. You are a World Changer! You may feel more like a diaper changer or an oil changer or but that is not your greatest calling. Your calling is to be a World Changer to those around you. So today, I want you to find a way to impact someone else's life.

Here are a few ideas:

☑ Leave someone a voice message or a text of encouragement.

☑ Buy someone's coffee for them.

☑ Offer to babysit a friend's child for an hour or so.

Just do something today! Take a moment to journal on the next page what you chose to do and how to felt to live bigger.

REFLECTION DAY

Day Twenty

RECORD: WHAT HAPPENED THIS WEEK FOR YOU?

_____

_____

_____

_____

_____

WHAT WAS YOUR PREVAILING EMOTION?

_____

_____

_____

_____

_____

_____

THOUGHT: WHAT DID YOU LEARN ABOUT YOURSELF

_____

_____

_____

_____

SKETCH: HOW WOULD YOU DRAW IT?

REFLECT: WHAT ARE YOU INVITING INTO YOUR LIFE WITH YOUR ACTIONS?

_____

_____

_____

_____

_____

CONCLUSION: IN ONE SENTENCE, WRITE YOUR MOST PROVOKING THOUGHT THAT WOULD MOVE YOU FORWARD:

_____

_____

_____

_____

_____

_____

FINAL
THOUGHTS

Living present to our purpose on the planet is leaping into love and spreading it around on anyone we come in contact with. It's acknowledging that we have one life to grow. Our roots and fruit will always tell the story. Leaping into Love is about embracing the process and the lifelong journey to know and be known by God.

In your pursuit of growing your spiritual life, consider adding one or more of the following resources to your library.

MORE RESOURCES BY HAVILAH

BOOKS AND BIBLE STUDIES

Eat, Pray, Hustle

I Do Hard Things

Radical Growth

Soul Food

The Good Stuff

Stronger Than The Struggle

ONLINE COURSES

Prophetic Personalities

Moms Of Men

Purpose eCourse

LEADERSHIP AND TRAINING

Message Prep
eCourse

Delivering A Message
eCourse

Truth to Table
Membership Community

FIND ALL OF THESE RESOURCES AND MORE AT
TRUTHTOTABLE.COM

STAY CONNECTED

▢ website *havilahcunnington.com*

ⓕ facebook *Havilah Cunnington*

ⓣ twitter *@mrshavilah*

ⓘ instagram *havilahcunnington*

▶ youtube *youtube.com/user/havilahcunnington*

@ email *info@havilahcunnington.com*

FOR MORE INFORMATION
visit havilahcunnington.com
or truthtotable.com

join our newsletter

REQUEST HAVILAH TO SPEAK

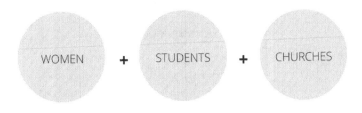

WOMEN + STUDENTS + CHURCHES

FOR
Retreats, conferences, one-night gatherings,
church services, leadership events

Made in the USA
Lexington, KY
22 February 2019